Praise for Sa

Sacred Work is a beacon of biblically based wisdom, inspiration, and guidance for any Christian woman navigating the challenges of leadership in the evolving professional world. As I turned the pages, I found myself captivated by Peggy's authenticity and vulnerability, sharing her personal journey with a transparency that makes her wisdom relatable and her insights actionable.
VANESSA JONES, vice president of lead management sales, Philips Image-Guided Therapy Devices

In *Sacred Work*, I love that Peggy Bodde not only shares her own experiences and learnings, but she also weaves in the stories and expertise of other women leaders. Collectively, these stories provide a rich tapestry of inspiration and practical tools to equip working women so they too can celebrate the sacredness of their work and be all God created them to be.
CATHERINE GATES, author of *The Confidence Cornerstone: A Woman's Guide to Fearless Leadership*; vice president of business partnerships, Polished Network

Sacred Work is a helpful playbook for female Christian leaders. Based on her extensive leadership experience, Peggy provides heartfelt advice and step-by-step instructions for managing crises, negotiating pay increases, recovering from failure, and more. Read this book to get your leadership questions answered!
DENISE LEE YOHN, founder and director, Faith & Work Journey

Whether you are a man or a woman, *Sacred Work* shines a light on challenges in the workplace today and provides practical steps in dealing with these challenges. Most importantly, Peggy provides biblical resources supporting her suggested solutions, and provides hope for what the workplace can become.
DIANE PADDISON, founder of 4word, and author of *Work, Love, Pray* and *Be Refreshed: A Year of Devotions for Women in the Workplace*

At a time when leaders need mentorship more than ever before, Peggy's words and heart shine through. In *Sacred Work*, you'll find spot-on and relatable wisdom that can be applied to all aspects of your leadership. Whether you're just stepping into the working world or a seasoned pro, her book has something to offer everyone—a breath of fresh air for those seeking encouragement and biblical mentorship.
ERIN BAXTER, director, marketing and communications, the Polished Network

The Christian working woman has been underserved for far too long. Thank you, Peggy, for pouring your life's work into a great resource to help women live out their calling in the workplace with excellence and a biblical perspective. Great job!

JIM BRANGENBERG, cohost and cofounder of iWork4Him

Using decades of experience as a corporate leader, mentor, and consultant, Peggy outlines the most pressing issues facing Christian women leaders. *Sacred Work* includes specific and practical ways women can overcome internal and external challenges to be more effective and confident leaders. Throughout the book, Peggy reminds her audience that secular work is a sacred calling and should be viewed as such. Her writing style is pragmatic and to the point, making it akin to John Maxwell's. *Sacred Work* is an essential virtual toolbox, and I'm buying a copy for every Christian woman leader I know!

JASON WOODWARD, operations executive and host of the *Biblical Leadership @ Work* podcast

Woohoo! Someone finally created a resource designed specifically for *Christian women* who have been called into leadership. I feel seen, encouraged, and equipped. This is the book my soul has been craving! *Sacred Work* is a road map for women aspiring to lead authentically, navigate challenges with grace, and make a lasting impact. Leaders at any level will benefit from Peggy's comprehensive "how to" guide for the most common leadership dilemmas they encounter!

KALI DAVIS, senior vice president at Harvest Group; Workmatters board member

Sacred Work is a resource destined for the bookshelf of every Christian working woman. Peggy has created a resource that is a great read from the first chapter to the last, but also a reference manual to turn to when we might have a specific issue that needs to be addressed. I now have access to tools that will allow God to do His sacred work in and through me.

MARTHA BRANGENBERG, cohost and cofounder of iWork4Him

Sacred Work is a must-read for every Christian leader. This book equips you to live your faith unapologetically as a leader in the marketplace. Peggy Bodde provides you with wisdom and insights on how to let your light shine for Jesus Christ as you face workplace challenges and embrace professional opportunities. *Sacred Work* will help you align your words and actions with your beliefs and will empower you to lead like Jesus.

NANCY J. LEWIS, president and founder of Progressive Techniques, Inc.

PEGGY BODDE

SACRED WORK

A CHRISTIAN WOMAN'S GUIDE TO LEADERSHIP IN THE MARKETPLACE

MOODY PUBLISHERS
CHICAGO

All Scripture quotations, unless otherwise indicated, are taken from the Holy Bible, New International Version®, NIV®. Copyright ©1973, 1978, 1984, 2011 by Biblica, Inc.™ Used by permission of Zondervan. All rights reserved worldwide. www.zondervan.com The "NIV" and "New International Version" are trademarks registered in the United States Patent and Trademark Office by Biblica, Inc.

Scripture quotations marked (NLT) are taken from the *Holy Bible*, New Living Translation, copyright ©1996, 2004, 2015 by Tyndale House Foundation. Used by permission of Tyndale House Publishers, Carol Stream, Illinois 60188. All rights reserved.

Some content in chapters 1 and 14 was previously published on the author's website.

Some persons depicted are compilations of individuals and situations. Other names and details have been changed to protect the privacy of individuals.

Published in association with Books & Such Literary Management, www.booksand such.com.

Edited by Pamela Joy Pugh
Interior design: Brandi Davis
Cover design: Erik M. Peterson
Author photo credit: Kierstan Renner

Library of Congress Cataloging-in-Publication Data

Names: Bodde, Peggy, author.
Title: Sacred work : a Christian woman's guide to leadership in the
   marketplace / Peggy Bodde.
Description: Chicago : Moody Publishers, [2024] | Includes bibliographical
   references. | Summary: "It's possible for women to be strong Christians
   and confident leaders. Mentor and longtime corporate leader Peggy Bodde
   views work as sacred and has invested her life in showing women how to
   thrive in the workplace. Peggy provides an invaluable and practical
   resource answering all your leadership challenges and questions"--
   Provided by publisher.
Identifiers: LCCN 2023039267 (print) | LCCN 2023039268 (ebook) | ISBN
   9780802432162 | ISBN 9780802472847 (ebook)
Subjects: LCSH: Christian women. | Christian leadership. | Leadership in
   women. | BISAC: RELIGION / Christian Living / Leadership & Mentoring |
   BUSINESS & ECONOMICS / Leadership
Classification: LCC BV4527 .B624 2024 (print) | LCC BV4527 (ebook) | DDC
   248.8/43--dc23/eng/20231122
LC record available at https://lccn.loc.gov/2023039267
LC ebook record available at https://lccn.loc.gov/2023039268

Originally delivered by fleets of horse-drawn wagons, the affordable paperbacks from D. L. Moody's publishing house resourced the church and served everyday people. Now, after more than 125 years of publishing and ministry, Moody Publishers' mission remains the same—even if our delivery systems have changed a bit. For more information on other books (and resources) created from a biblical perspective, go to www.moodypublishers .com or write to:

Moody Publishers
820 N. LaSalle Boulevard
Chicago, IL 60610

1 3 5 7 9 10 8 6 4 2

Printed in the United States of America

For Ma and Pa Brown
God shaped the best of me using strong women leaders, Ma.
You were the first.

To the Goldings, Scalettas, Wests,
and George—
I'm so glad you're mine.

Contents

Your Work Matters to God

Have you ever wondered if your work matters to God?

I remember being at a social event years ago with people from my church community. I was a single mom and a corporate leader, and these events made me nervous; I felt like I didn't fit in. That day, I heard innocent comments like, "I'm sorry you have to work and can't stay home with your daughter." And "God gifted you as a leader. You should do something that makes a difference for Him, like working in ministry or missions." My insecurity chewed on these words, and I left early, with big question marks around the most important areas of my life.

Later, I labored in prayer over doubts I couldn't seem to shake. I felt less-than as a mom and a Christian, and I was sure God was disappointed in my career choice. Maybe people were right. How could I possibly make a difference for God as a leader in the market-place? Maybe I'd misunderstood my calling to lead.

Suddenly, the Holy Spirit interrupted. "Who are you listening to? Because it's not Me."

That was my turning point. I realized God doesn't live inside a compartment labeled "sacred." He lives in *us*, and we carry the sacredness that comes from Him everywhere we go, including the workplace.

There are more women leaders, managers, and professionals in the workforce now than ever before, and you're part of that growing number. This is cause for celebration, but women are also time-starved, stressed, and tired. They often feel alone in their professional struggles and doubt that their struggles are legitimate. Many feel torn about embracing who they are as Christians while thriving as leaders. Are any of these feelings familiar?

Living out your faith in the workplace is important to you, but you're not sure what that looks like. Perhaps you're torn about embracing who you are as a Christian while thriving as a leader. One seems to compromise the other, which leaves you feeling conflicted, discouraged, and not enough.

Maybe you feel isolated, or you wish you had a mentor, but you don't have time to find one. When you have to confront conflict or you're passed over for a promotion, you want to respond in a way that honors your faith, but how? What about disagreements with your boss or when a coworker betrays you? How do you respond as a follower of Jesus?

As a Christian woman who spent twenty-five years as a corporate leader, I've experienced the same tension and questions. You're not alone! I understand how you feel, and I talk to women weekly who express these same frustrations and doubts. I want you to know and embrace this truth: it's possible for women to be strong Christians and confident business leaders. We don't have to sacrifice one to become the other. This is the message I share with women through my foundation, Sacred Work, and it's one I want to share with you in this book.

Throughout my career, I had trouble finding Christian women mentors or even finding resources about leadership written by women for women. So I decided to become for others what I didn't have. I prayed for opportunities to come alongside women and help them grow professionally, and with every woman I mentored, my passion for this pursuit grew.

After I left the corporate world, I knew God didn't want me to waste the decades of business experience He'd given me. So I started the Sacred Work Foundation to provide free career and leadership coaching for women. This book is an extension of the foundation; think of it as your pocket-sized mentor. Chapters and sections are designed to be stand-alone as needed.

Are you battling imposter syndrome? Struggling with remote leadership? Each chapter addresses pain points that have been identified as the most relevant and pressing in the lives of female Christian leaders today. You can quickly turn to the chapter you need when you need it, or you can read the book straight through. Either way, you'll find practical strategies, doable steps, and biblical guidance. Each chapter ends with a section called "Sacred Work," where you'll find God's Word and a big dose of biblical encouragement, because when you equip your faith, you equip your leadership.

God loves and values you, and He values your work as a leader. You are set apart for His service, and you don't lose that part of your identity when you go to work. If anything, it becomes more important as you face demanding challenges and lead the people you've been entrusted with. God is here for you, and I am here for you. Welcome to this space, dear leader.

1

Recognizing and Overcoming Imposter Syndrome

Your identity is secure when you believe
that what God says about you is true.[1]

NONA JONES, CHIEF CONTENT AND PARTNERSHIPS OFFICER, YOUVERSION

I once helped a young professional prepare to interview for a promotion at her company. "Beth" had a documented history of stellar performance in addition to leadership experience, and she was excited about growing with her organization. Besides the standard interview prep, she created a 30/60/90-day plan outlining goals for each stage of the new job. If that wasn't impressive enough, she also wrote a one-page project proposal to increase employee engagement while simultaneously improving client satisfaction. Beth practiced for the interview, prepared her questions and documents in advance, and felt confident about her chances of getting the job. The interview went well, and I wasn't surprised a week later when she called to tell me they offered her the position. What *did* surprise me was how she sounded.

Her excitement and confidence were gone, and instead of a person who had just received a promotion, she was anxious and doubtful. As we talked, she said things like:

> "I'm not sure I'm the best person for the job."
>
> "I don't think I'm qualified to handle these extra responsibilities."
>
> "They should have given the job to someone with better credentials."

Unfortunately, what Beth experienced isn't an unknown phenomenon: imposter syndrome had made an appearance. Understanding what it is, where it may come from, and how it affects us frees us to overcome it. Scripture tells us God values, loves, and accepts us. But because we live in an imperfect world, complicated factors can interfere with our ability to hear that truth. In this chapter, we'll take those factors apart and look at ways to reclaim God's truth about who we are.

WHAT IS IMPOSTER SYNDROME?

Psychology Today explains that "people who struggle with imposter syndrome believe that they are undeserving of their achievements and the high esteem in which they are, in fact, generally held. They feel that they aren't as competent or intelligent as others might think—and that soon enough, people will discover the truth about them."[2] Women who suffer from imposter syndrome downplay workplace recognition and achievement and see others as more qualified than themselves.

You may be experiencing imposter syndrome if you:

- are a woman of color working in a colorless company[3]
- are a woman working in a male-dominated industry
- have been a minority in your workplace for most of your career
- were overlooked at work for a long time before being recognized
- had a childhood where performance was emphasized but nothing was ever good enough
- were raised in an environment where women were not encouraged to pursue careers or become leaders
- place extreme pressure on yourself not to fail
- battle perfectionism, comparison, and workaholism

When I started my business career in the 1990s, very few women worked in the outdoor industry, where companies promoted outdoor exploration and activities. This unique group of businesses had even fewer women leaders, which created feelings of isolation. I experienced moments when I felt like Beth did, even before I knew what to call it. It seemed absurd, but even positive events triggered feelings of fraud and insecurity, such as career changes, promotions, or being recognized. Did I really deserve the _____ [promotion, raise, recognition]? At other times, negative situations happened and brought out the same feelings.

Once, while I was working with potential suppliers in a closed-door meeting, one of the executives barged in, interrupting us. He told me to have the receptionist order new urinal filters because he didn't like the smell of the existing ones. Being treated disrespectfully led to self-doubt about my value to the company. But as many women do, I stuffed my response—emotional and otherwise—and told myself to toughen up. I've since realized that if we can't name a problem, we can't confront it. And if we don't confront it, we can't overcome it.

Women struggle with imposter syndrome more than men, and psychologists think this is largely because of cultural and societal norms. When women make strides in a direction that flows opposite of their upbringing or what they see and experience around them, imposter syndrome is likely to show up. They experience an underlying sense that they don't belong and aren't qualified to be where they are, regardless of experience, education, or competency.

> We tend to dismiss our feelings, but one of the first steps to overcoming imposter syndrome is to face our feelings and share our struggles.

For these same reasons, women of color are very susceptible to experiencing imposter syndrome. Clinical psychologist Emily Hu says, "We're more likely to experience imposter syndrome if we don't see many examples of people who look like us or share our background who are clearly succeeding in our field."[4]

Lean In, a US organization that helps women pursue their work ambitions, reported in 2022 that "for every 100 men promoted from entry level to manager, only 87 women are promoted, and only 82 women of color are promoted." The same report showed that "only 1 in 4 C-suite executives is a woman, and only 1 in 20 is a woman of color."[5]

Statistics and studies like these are helpful because they validate and reframe what we're experiencing. We tend to dismiss our feelings, but one of the first steps to overcoming imposter syndrome is to face our feelings and share our struggles. Talking about this topic may make us feel more vulnerable, but God designed us to be in community! We need each other, and I'm glad you're here.

What's the Big Deal About Imposter Syndrome?

Experiencing imposter syndrome and *not* confronting it creates outcomes that stop you from fulfilling your professional goals and reaching your leadership potential:

1. Instead of being excited about a new job or position, you waste time and energy wondering if you're a diversity hire or if you fooled everyone into believing your qualifications. When you first step into a new job or role, the energy and focus you bring are critical. You can't afford to be distracted by doubt.
2. You may under-assess your worth, so you don't require others to treat you fairly or with respect. This can hold you back from asking for the raises or promotions you deserve. You feel less-than, so you accept less.
3. Instead of graciously and confidently accepting praise, recognition, or even a new title, you resist and deflect. Responding this way demeans your professionalism and looks like false humility.

IMPOSTER SYNDROME AND CHRISTIANS

I was a corporate leader for decades and now mentor women leaders through my foundation, Sacred Work. Based on my experience and what I hear from others, Christian women are more prone to imposter syndrome. Not only are we going against broad cultural norms by filling positions formerly held by men, but we may also be going against norms established in our faith communities. A prevalent evangelical movement in the 1980s and early 1990s framed a woman's place as being in the home.[6] Many Christian women were raised in legalistic homes or within a gender stereotype that didn't include being assertive, leading people, or pursuing a career. These pressure points come together and cause women to face imposter syndrome in two realms: as Christians and as leaders. Comparison then becomes a frequent guest.

In her book *Unconditioned Love*, Staci Diffendaffer describes the experience like this: "I tried to transform into who I thought these women were because they seemed like *the right kind* of Christian women. And while I admired them for being *the right kind* of Christian women, a small resentment started to form. If I am different from them, that must mean that I am not *the right kind* of Christian woman. I reasoned that I wouldn't be accepted if I was just . . . me."[7]

> **The absence of other women leaders in my world created a question mark. I couldn't find firm footing in business or faith circles.**

At times we question if being a female leader in a secular workplace is a godly pursuit. Maybe we misunderstood God's direction in our lives, and we shouldn't be working outside the home at all. Or we're ambivalent because we're not limiting our leadership to church roles. We crack open Christian leadership books for women and find that most are about women who lead ministries, which seems to affirm we're in the wrong place. People in the Christian community may have said silly things to us, like:

"Leadership isn't a calling. It's a vocation."

"Leadership can't be a calling because you get paid to do it."

"Leadership is a job, not a purpose."

In church circles, I saw myself as the odd person out. I was a single mom when I started my career and often felt less-than because I was the sole provider and worked outside the home. I enjoyed my work and loved leading people, which led to guilt and angst. When other women asked me about my job, I felt like I had to apologize because I enjoyed it and was grateful for it.

I also didn't have access to women leaders as mentors. Women who led or managed in the workplace were scarce, and I couldn't even find a leadership book in Barnes and Noble written by a woman! The absence of other women leaders in my world created a question mark. I couldn't find firm footing in business *or* faith circles. Leadership in the corporate world wasn't laying out welcome mats for women, and the Christian world wasn't offering examples or affirmations that women in workplace leadership should have a seat at the table. Thankfully, cultural and societal norms are changing and continuing to evolve.

What about you? Do you ever find yourself in work situations where you struggle to fit into the role of "Christian" versus "leader," and then you wonder if you're qualified for either? You may feel torn between your identity as a Christian woman and your identity as a leader. It may even seem like you have to choose one over the other, and that tension chips away at your confidence. Despite your education, your work history, and all your best efforts—your doubts pile up, and you toss them into a big box at the back of your mind labeled "I don't belong here."

> *Maybe I'm a fake leader. Maybe I'm a fake Christian.*
>
> *Why do I feel undone, unworthy, and unqualified?*
>
> *Why do I resist being recognized for my leadership or acknowledged for my faith?*
>
> *I don't think I'm cut out to be a leader.*
>
> *If I were a stronger Christian, I wouldn't have this struggle.*
>
> *How do I overcome the fear that I'll fail in both places?*

As a corporate leader, I experienced the same questions and uncertainty. There's a reason for that. Satan isn't creative: he's predictable and repetitive. The ruler of this world always wants less for us than the Ruler of our hearts. Satan uses voices from the past and present to create shadows around our light, and these distractions bog us down. We begin to doubt where God has placed us and the leadership talent He's given us.

From Scripture, we know the enemy stirs up confusion to immobilize us. If we thrive as Christian women and leaders, Satan has plenty to lose, so he peddles the lie that we're double agents with no standing in either space. But you're here, which means your eyes are open to the struggle behind your smile and successes. Hopefully, you now understand more about what imposter syndrome is and why it exists.

In her book *Killing Comparison*, Nona Jones says, "Knowing what your insecure foundations are is important because once you know what they are, you can do something about them."[8]

Let's take that next step!

HOW TO OVERCOME IMPOSTER SYNDROME

Imposter syndrome has deep roots growing from seeds planted deep down and cultivated without our knowledge. They may have started in childhood or along our career paths, and they were watered every time we were overlooked, underrepresented, or marginalized. Gradually, massive weeds of insecurity crowded out our confidence. But regardless of why or how imposter syndrome affects you, you can take steps to weed it out:

- Take control of your thoughts, so they don't take control of you. Psychology experts estimate that the average person has over 6,000 thoughts in one day.[9] We have the power to choose what we think about, so make sure your thoughts are serving you well. Be mindful of thoughts that suggest you're in any way undeserving or not the "real deal." When you recognize negative thought patterns, take action against them. There are lots of suggestions below!

- Write a list of Bible verses affirming who God says you are and keep it where you can see it daily. One of my favorites is Romans 8:37, "No, in all these things we are more than conquerors through him who loved us." It reminds me I'm loved and victorious!

- Keep a file of your professional achievements including awards, promotion letters, complimentary emails, and accomplishments from performance reviews. When you sense doubts about your competence creeping in, read through the file.

- Write a positive reminder and keep it in a private place that's quickly accessible, like under a keyboard. Choose words that stifle the negative self-talk that gets stirred up when imposter syndrome is triggered. For example, mine is, "I worked hard to get here. I belong here. God created me to do this work in this place."

- Talk to a trusted friend. Women who know you and care for you are priceless resources. It's freeing to share your thoughts with another person who will listen and respond with your best interest in mind. Friends can speak the truth against doubts you have about your abilities.

- Journal your thoughts when you feel anxious or doubtful about your strengths and accomplishments. Use these questions to get started: What event happened immediately before the negative spiral? What feelings did you experience? When was the last time you felt this way in your career? What do the two instances have in common? Answering these questions helps you pinpoint triggers and uncover root causes. Journal entries are also helpful when talking about your experiences with friends, mentors, or therapists.

• Work with a mentor or therapist to discover how imposter syndrome may have developed, what your specific triggers are, and how to further overcome them.

Take courage! Ask the Holy Spirit to increase your awareness, so you know when imposter syndrome is happening. He is our guide and advocate, and He will help you overcome. Start with small steps and keep going!

SACRED WORK

An often-quoted verse in Esther reads, "And who knows if perhaps you were made queen for just such a time as this?" (Est. 4:14b NLT). God's presence is all over Esther's story, even though His name is never mentioned once. Esther is in the minority as a Jew and a woman in a Persian palace where their ways are not her ways, her commitment to her beliefs is tested, and she has to overcome many challenges.

She struggles with her confidence as a Jewish woman and her power as a queen. We can almost imagine her thoughts:

"Am I more than just another pretty face?"

"Will my uncle and the Jewish people doubt my beliefs and convictions?"

"How can I live out my faith in this environment?"

"Am I really qualified to plead a case when lives are on the line?"

God takes an inexperienced orphan girl, whose identity and background make her the perfect candidate to become the queen of Persia, and He uses her to save His people. This story holds unique encouragement for us as Christian women in the workplace. Like us, Esther probably experienced doubts about her qualifications and her identity as a woman of God. But just as she was perfectly qualified for the job at hand, you are too. You are exactly who and where God intended you to be.

When you feel conflicted or inadequate, remember this: who we are as followers of Christ informs who we are as leaders of people. Faith and leadership work together; they are not at odds with each other. Our identity and calling are secure in Him, and we can lean into that truth when imposter syndrome threatens an appearance. God created you to follow Him, and He created you to lead.

My prayer for you: Thank You, Father, for the woman who is reading this. Thank You that she bravely carries Your banner into all areas of her life, including the workplace. Help her remember that her identity in You is true and secure. Heal her from past situations that weaken her confidence, and give her strength and courage as she fights against self-doubt.

2

Making Difficult Decisions

Wherever you see a successful business,
someone once made a courageous decision.[1]

PETER DRUCKER, AUTHOR AND FOUNDER OF THE DRUCKER INSTITUTE

M y first corporate job was in the early 1990s, before Wi-Fi
and smartphones were part of the everyday business
world. Not long after I was hired, my boss, Steve, went on a work
trip and I fielded a call in his absence. His assistant knew all the ins
and outs of the business, but she was at home sick. The caller was
from the exhibit hall for our industry trade show and explained that
"today" was our "last chance" to confirm our booth space before the
price increased by $5,000. An extra $5,000 was a lot of money, and
when I heard "last chance," I panicked. I took the caller's info and
promised to call her back by the end of the day.

I shuffled through Steve's desk again, checked his (paper) calendar,
and tried once more to reach him by phone. No answer. When I asked
around the company, I was met with a lot of shrugged shoulders. He
was also my first business mentor, and I didn't want to disappoint him.

At the end of the day, I was out of time. I paced around and finally called the exhibit hall, saying I couldn't confirm our booth space.

The next morning Steve called, and when I told him what happened, he said we were indeed supposed to have a booth at the trade show; it was the most important show of the year. I gulped. Here I was, two months on the job at a small company, and I'd just cost him $5,000. His car phone was about to lose service, so he said we'd talk about what happened later, and he ended with this, "Don't worry. I'd rather you move forward with a wrong decision than wait around for me to tell you the right one."

Once back in the office, Steve helped me understand the details about the trade show. Technically, we had a contract giving us until the end of the month to secure our booth space. I hadn't cost the company $5,000 after all! He showed me where the contracts were and taught me how to review them. I learned that the urgent call was merely a ploy to push for a commitment, so the exhibit hall could find out early how many empty spaces they needed to fill. Most of all, I learned that making a decision is more important than making a mistake.

> The pressure is clearly on leaders to decide what's best for their companies and to be right much of the time. There are many tools to help with the process.

As my leadership responsibilities increased throughout my career, I came to realize that stakes grow along with responsibilities. You may have experienced this realization yourself. There's no room for uncertain leaders who waffle in their choices. We're criticized if we take too long to decide or if we decide in haste, and the consequences of either can be far-reaching. The burden of good judgment is heavy to bear, but it's a quality both employers and employees expect leaders to have. An article by *Forbes* describes decision-making as "the one leadership quality that you need."[2]

Just how quantifiable is this quality? McKinsey & Company uses numbers to put this into perspective: "Ineffective decision making has significant implications for company productivity. On average, respondents spend 37 percent of their time making decisions, and more than half of this time was thought to be spent ineffectively. For managers at an average Fortune 500 company, this could translate into more than 530,000 days of lost working time and roughly $250 million of wasted labor costs per year."[3]

The pressure is clearly on leaders to decide what's best for their companies and to be right much of the time. There are many tools to help with the process, including a leader's core values. For example, my first business mentor valued humility and empowerment. Because of this, he took responsibility for what I decided in his absence. He didn't criticize what I had done and instead used the situation to teach and empower me. His values guided his choices.

I recently caught up with my friend Amy Lively, and she shared her own story about leadership values and decision-making.

VALUES AND DECISION-MAKING

Amy co-owns The Lively Merchant with her husband, David, and their employees work remotely across the United States. Amy explained why their company established a remote work environment from its inception. David's long-term vision was to access the best talent while providing employees with rewarding careers and flexible schedules. He wanted to build a business focused on the value of serving employees and their clients, so that's exactly what they did.

Even though this successful husband-and-wife team has had remote workers in place since 2007, their decision-making skills came under pressure when COVID-19 hit. Amy and I chatted about the choices they faced because I was curious about their decision-making strategies during the pandemic.

The Lively Merchant develops e-commerce websites for customers who also have brick-and-mortar stores. In March 2020, the company went from thriving in a robust economy to fielding numerous customer cancellations a day. During their initial meetings, Amy, David, and their leadership team discussed laying people off or reducing positions to part-time.

After spending several days in prayer and conversation with trusted mentors, they decided to push forward instead of shrinking back. They stopped talking about layoffs and instead brainstormed ways to involve all their employees in helping customers, and the company, survive. This option was the opposite of what many other businesses chose, but Amy and David were at peace with it because it was in alignment with their values—to serve their employees and clients.

The leadership team created a plan and engaged every person in the company to make it happen. Regardless of department or position, employees reached out to customers. They didn't pretend they had all the answers but instead said something like this: "We haven't been through this before, but here are some effective actions businesses are taking. We want to offer them to you and see how we can serve you." Then they helped clients customize their websites so brick-and-mortar shoppers would know how businesses were handling COVID-19.

Instead of losing customers, existing customers started adding services. In addition, potential clients who had been undecided about having websites moved forward. The company grew, employees thrived, and so did the customers they served. Amy and David didn't set out to grow their company when COVID-19 surfaced. They were more concerned with living out their foundational value of serving.

This value informed their preference to expand efforts during a time when cutting back was the norm, and exponential growth was simply an unexpected (and welcome) outcome.

At the end of our conversation, I asked Amy to summarize how she viewed a leader's role in decision-making. She used this analogy:

> Leaders who shy away from decision-making are like thermometers. They look at circumstances and note that temperatures are dropping or rising, but they don't respond to what they see. Proactive leaders are more like thermostats; they note the drops and rises and *respond* by making choices. Acknowledging the reality of what's going on isn't enough; leaders have to go beyond this step. Biblical, godly principles like praying and seeking wise counsel help leaders use good judgment and make wise choices.[4]

Reflection: Before you're faced with the next tough choice at work, I invite you to take a few minutes and think about these questions: What are your values? How can you use them to guide your decision-making? What would it look like for your preferences to honor your values?

WOMEN AND DECISION-MAKING

Did you know that as a woman, your role as a decider is an important part of why you're a strong corporate leader? Your ability to make hard choices gives your company a competitive advantage. It's your superpower!

Neuroscientists agree women are equipped to decide in ways men aren't. In normal day-to-day situations, men and women process choices in similar ways. But under duress, men and women decide differently because their brains operate differently.[5] In the business world, stress is commonplace for leaders, and evidence suggests that women are well-equipped to swim in these deep waters.

Women tend to look for creative alternatives and are curious about other people's ideas.

Women operate well under pressure. There's a perception that women's feelings interfere with logical decision-making, but multiple studies contradict this perception.[6] Neuroscientists have found that when men are in high-pressure situations, they take bigger risks.[7] They are less able to assess risk levels and potential losses because they become focused on the biggest gains.[8] Women's brains, however, process stress differently, so they make less risky decisions in demanding circumstances.[9] They're able to think through potential outcomes more clearly and logically.[10]

Women are more likely to include and consider others. Another perception is that because women often choose a cooperative approach, they lack confidence or are indecisive. Research explains the true reasoning behind this approach:

The *Harvard Business Review* interviewed eighteen organizations to evaluate how women decide differently from men. Research found that men tend to approach decision-making competitively and lean toward what's in the best interest of just one party.[11] They're also more prone to decide based on cultural norms within the company, such as how things have always been done.[12] This same study showed women are more likely to consider and balance conflicting interests. They look for creative alternatives and are curious about other people's ideas.[13]

According to the study, women want to understand how an option will impact other people or departments. They embrace consensus building and value fairness and collaboration over authority.[14]

Scientific studies represent generalizations, but they help us understand how men and women approach choices differently. It's empowering to note that research supports women as effective deciders—this is a fact you can return to when you doubt yourself. Remember, too, that God created men and women as equal but unique beings. Both genders bring different strengths to the decision-making table.

THE DECISION-MAKING PROCESS

The more significant the outcome, the more difficult it is to make the best choice. Leaders may become overwhelmed by demands to make the right choice at the right time. Pressure builds and can lead to delays and indecision. But every choice comes down to two scenarios:

1. You can be decisive and control the outcome.
2. You can be indecisive and react to the outcome.

You may not realize this, but doing nothing is a decision. Making tough calls is a non-negotiable part of the job. Here are nine practical steps to help you get started.

The Nine-Step Process

A reliable process helps you make wise choices. When you're faced with tough decisions, processes provide guardrails. They help you organize information, identify alternatives, and maintain focus. Processes also save time because they act like the GPS in your car, telling you where to go next. You'll gain clarity and confidence as you move through each step.

1. **Clarify the decision that needs to be made.** Use these questions to gain a clearer understanding: What do you hope or need to accomplish? What's the goal or purpose? What problem do you want to solve?

2. **Use your core values, and those of your company, as a lens.** Highlight options that are strongly aligned with these values and eliminate options that don't align.

3. **Assess your personal toolbox.** What wisdom, experience, and industry knowledge can help you? Are you lacking in any of these areas? How can you supplement what's missing with external resources?

4. **Consult external resources.** Leveraging knowledge outside your company will help expand your thinking. What evidence and data can inform your selection? What research and facts can you gather? How many experts outside your organization can you talk to?

5. **Collect *all* the options.** This means thinking outside the limitations of your own bias and perspective. Don't seek feedback only from people you're confident will agree with you. Listen to viewpoints and ideas that differ from yours. The most insightful revelations come out of healthy discord.

6. **Involve other people.** Spend time with people who understand the significance of different options better than you do. Talk through the pros and cons with employees who will be impacted by your decision.

7. **Weigh the evidence.** Document and organize the options, along with opinions, data points, arguments, and probable outcomes. Assess each alternative against the need, goal, or purpose you identified in Step 1. Talk through and reflect on which has the highest potential for success and which aligns the most closely with the company's core values—and yours.

8. **Act.** Choose the best option and act on it. Communicate what you've decided, develop an implementation plan, and then execute it.

9. **Reflect on the decision.** After a reasonable amount of time, invite employees to weigh in on how the decision is affecting them. Ask yourself if you solved the problem, answered the question, or met the goal. Be accountable for the consequences, even if it means reworking some steps or trying a different option.

Strategies That Will Help

Besides the nine-step process, these strategies will help you make hard decisions too:

Trust your intuition. Don't dismiss gut feelings. Your intuition is a powerful tool because it's composed of data that includes memories, lessons learned, the company's needs, and your individual preferences.[15] All this information coincides with your ability to analyze and weigh options, becoming one more tool that helps you make important choices.

Acknowledge your personal biases. Leaders try to be objective, but every person brings some type of bias to the table. Recognizing biases will help you better understand how they could sway your selections. Then you can take measures to outsmart yourself!

For example, I've historically been protective of the people I lead. This is a strength, but it can also get in the way. Since I know this about myself, I take measures to defuse defensiveness, which otherwise might skew my choices. When I need to make a decision that affects my team, I know my tendency is to defend. So I force myself to have an open mind and a closed mouth when I'm listening to views that differ from mine. I also filter different perspectives through people I trust.

Lean toward moderate over extreme. Pressure can push leaders into making quick, extreme choices. To be objective, take yourself out of the red zone. If a decision is urgent, your short-term impulses may become problematic and interfere with your ability to choose wisely. Unless it's an emergency, press pause and step away. Come back to the process after your brain and emotions have rested.

In pressing situations, create distance by imagining how you'll feel about your choice an hour after you've made it. Then imagine how you'll feel tomorrow, next month, and next year. This exercise helps you rebalance your emotions, so you're aware of their presence but not being led by them.

Maintain humility. Don't assume you know all the outcomes without input from other people or sources. Pride leads you to make a selection without exploring all the potential consequences. It also influences you to rely too heavily on past successes, even though yesterday's solutions aren't always the answer to today's problems. Being humble means welcoming other people into the process and being curious about their ideas. You recognize that choosing wisely is your responsibility, but you also know that you're wiser together than alone.

Make yourself accountable from the beginning. The more difficult the decision, the more likely it is to drag out. Leaders don't want to upset employees or disrupt the work environment, and they definitely don't want to fail. So they procrastinate. To avoid delays, give yourself a deadline by which you'll have done certain steps in the process or by which you'll have a conclusion. Share this information with someone else: human resources, your boss, a peer, or an employee.

SACRED WORK

In Jesus' time, rabbis used a specific way of teaching called *remez*, a Hebrew term meaning "hint."[16] Jesus and other rabbis quoted Scripture to their students, who tried to remember where else they had heard similar themes or concepts. They asked questions like these: Have we heard this before? Where else has this shown up in Scripture?[17]

Through discussions, listeners connected the teaching to a broader meaning. *Remez* would take them on a trip back in time to Scriptures and lessons where themes had occurred before—connecting points. For example, *remez* helped me see a biblical theme of the greater coming to the lesser: God sending prophets and, ultimately, Jesus to help and save us. And then Jesus seeking out His disciples and telling parables about the good shepherd seeking out one lost sheep.

This way of interpreting Scripture relied on people pausing to ask questions and search for connections,[18] and an important part of the pause was in the looking back. The next time you need to make an important decision, pause and consider past situations that required you to make challenging choices. Difficult personal choices might include deciding which degree to pursue, choosing a city to live in, or buying your first home. Maybe you pivoted careers or switched companies or industries. As a leader, you've likely decided when to fire someone or how flexible your team's schedule will be.

Brainstorm as many prior decisions as you can and write them out. Then circle the ones with positive results. Take a minute to look at the circles on the page. These circles show that you're building a track record of good choices. You aren't being asked to do something completely new to you. You're a decider, and you've had success with it!

Now time yourself for five minutes. Next to each circled decision, reflect and record how you chose the best option. When the time is up, note any patterns and connections in the way you make decisions. This exercise of looking back is eye-opening because it can show you what you're already doing right. What an encouragement to see how God has guided you from stepping stone to stepping stone. You can count on His presence through every decision you make, and you can make choices with confidence because He equips you:

> "If any of you lacks wisdom, you should ask God, who gives generously to all without finding fault, and it will be given to you" (James 1:5).

3

Managing Workplace Conflict

There is an immutable conflict at work in life and in business:
a constant battle between peace and chaos. Neither can be mastered,
but both can be influenced. How you go about that is the key to success.[1]

PHIL KNIGHT, NIKE COFOUNDER AND FORMER CEO

One of my new managers, "Sarah," became frustrated because her employee, "Dan," was causing friction in the department. Dan was also new and had been hired by the previous manager. He complained about customers once he got off the phone with them, yet he spent an excessive amount of time chatting with them about his personal life. The team sat in an open workspace, so everyone could hear him.

Sarah came to me frustrated about the complaints and the employee himself. Her desk wasn't near Dan's, but she made it a point to listen whenever she was close by. She also checked the phone logs, which verified the excessive time Dan spent on calls.

She said, "I dread coming in to work because of this issue. It's been going on for weeks, and I had hoped Dan was just going through a hard time and that this was temporary. I hear the phone ring at his desk and cringe. When I walk through the team's work area, I feel everyone staring at me. They expect me to handle it."[2]

"Yes," I told her. "They expect you to handle it, and so do I."

The insignificant problems you ignore today become big disruptions tomorrow. Workplace strife requires managers and leaders to act. The longer we wait, the harsher the consequences are. Here are five tips I shared with Sarah:

1. **Conflict is normal.** Whether it's between employees, leaders, or departments, arguments are bound to happen.

2. **Remember that it's your job.** Managing conflict is what you're paid to do. When you're in charge, you're responsible for minimizing and defusing differences.

3. **Think about the consequences.** If you don't act, you'll see morale, productivity, and your reputation degrade. You also contribute to a culture where accountability loses its place. Employees will talk among themselves until the issue escalates and becomes disruptive.

4. **Imagine what life on the other side of the conflict looks like.** This step has always been a prime motivator for me. I asked Sarah, "Can you imagine what it would be like to have this burden off your back? Wouldn't it be great to walk through the office feeling confident because you took care of a dilemma instead of feeling ashamed because you hadn't?"

5. **Know that when you manage conflict well, you're building a stronger, better workplace.** Your employees will respect you as their leader. They'll feel safe coming to you because they know you'll do what's required so they can thrive. You build trust.

Sarah privately confronted her employee and clarified which behaviors needed to change. The behaviors did *not* change, causing the problem to resurface. But this time, Sarah was prepared. She had gained traction and confidence by confronting Dan the first time. He didn't receive the correction well and left the company.

It was a tough experience for a new manager, but because of it, Sarah grew as a leader and forged a strong relationship with her team. Unhealthy tension dissipated and the team dynamic changed for the better.

WHY IS IT IMPORTANT TO DEAL
WITH CONFLICT QUICKLY?

As you know, managing misunderstandings can be a daily event: A colleague makes irreversible decisions, causing fallout for other departments. Employees create tension because their communication styles are prickly, but they don't seem concerned about the impact. Stress, office politics, and clashing personalities complicate the strife.

These scenarios are wearing, and even seasoned leaders struggle. There's a reason for that: addressing dissension is complex and often unpleasant. But how and when leaders respond will determine whether the outcome is constructive or destructive and whether relationships become stronger or more divided.

Proverbs 15:1 reads, "A gentle answer turns away wrath, but a harsh word stirs up anger." In this verse, the Hebrew word *wrath* means "a burning anger or rage."[3] When a disagreement comes into our purview, we become the "gentle answer" that keeps the anger from spreading and the rage from growing. We have two responsibilities when wrath shows up: the first is to answer or respond and the second is to do so in a way that takes the heat down by several degrees. Bringing calm into a disagreement is the first step toward people and business returning to their best versions.

CPP, Inc., the publisher of the Myers-Briggs assessment, defines workplace conflict as "any workplace disagreement that disrupts the flow of work,"[4] and this disruption affects organizations and individuals. Two people or departments may think an argument is only between them, but the tension radiates outward. Work stops moving forward and people stop enjoying their work. The impact is exponential when leaders fail to intervene. Women I've mentored from different companies shared these examples with me:

- Two people vie for the same promotion, and surrounding departments split into two camps, each for one candidate and against the other. Respective leaders observe the behavior but deem it normal and let it go.
- A team member talks about politics before meetings start. The rest of the team is irritated. Some disagree with her, and others don't want to hear about politics at work. Talking about non-work topics before meetings is commonplace, so the project manager hesitates to say anything.
- An employee constantly complains and naysays other people's ideas. He's a top performer, but his behavior drags the department down. His manager writes it off as a personality difference and ignores it.
- A sales director makes decisions that negatively impact the operations and logistics departments. Departmental leaders address the problem once but drop the issue when the director doesn't change.

Lies We Tell Ourselves About Dealing With Conflict

In each of the above scenarios, leaders chose the path of least resistance. They rationalized inaction or lost their motivation when first efforts failed. As a result, each predicament will fester. We've all experienced circumstances when we needed to quell contention or circle back to unresolved problems, but we didn't. When this happens, we feel worse over time. We know we should act because it's our responsibility, yet we delay. Why? Here are a few lies we tell ourselves:

> Confronting people further weakens the relationships of everyone involved.
>
> The squabble is overwhelming everyone. It's better to wait until things settle down.
>
> Calling attention to the disagreement just makes matters worse.
>
> Eventually, the issue will resolve itself.
>
> Performance is more important than personality.

All these false rationalizations give us permission to delay action or not to act at all. The number one reason we let this happen is we don't like confrontation. Even the word *confrontation* evokes a negative emotional reaction. We feel uncomfortable, so we skirt around the tension. But skirting what's uncomfortable comes at the expense of doing what's necessary—an expense paid by the organization, and everyone involved. The truth is that confrontation creates short-term discomfort for long-term gains.

ADDRESS CONFLICT HEAD-ON

Here are four reasons you can't afford to ignore workplace conflict:

1. Avoiding conflict erodes trust and dissolves your credibility as a leader. Being liked is optional; being responsible is not.

2. Contention is disruptive. Employees stop focusing on their jobs and become fixated on the infighting.
3. Bickering is divisive. Whether the battle is between departments, team members, or leaders, employees either take sides willingly or feel pressured to do so.
4. The longer discord is ignored, the more toxic the workplace becomes.

These are all negative outcomes, but positive outcomes are equally possible. Catherine Gates, the executive director of Women in the Marketplace,[5] reminds us that positive outcomes are achievable if we manage dissension with the right mindset. She describes how to shift your perspective and the benefits that can result:

> Look at every disagreement as an opportunity to build a relationship. As you seek to understand the other person's perspective, you get to know them better. When you ask questions and take time to listen and learn, you develop a better connection. Over time, you build trust. You learn how to present and speak into the person's framework more effectively. They see the effort you're making, and, in time, they become more receptive and willing to cooperate.[6]

Keeping the positive possibilities in mind is important because conflict resolution is weighty business. Other positive outcomes include:

> Stronger, healthier work cultures
> Deeper trust in leadership
> More innovative solutions
> Improved communication skills
> Better emotional intelligence

Deep breath! If you're reading this, you're probably in the midst of messiness and seeking a way through. You may have read one of the "what not to do" scenarios that struck a little too close for comfort. I get it because much of what I've learned has come the hard way. I've procrastinated, overreacted, underreacted, and flat-out dropped the ball (see chapter 10 on failure). It's never too late to learn. You'll get better at resolving conflict and doing it will get easier. I believe in you, and you can do this!

HOW DO WE AVOID TAKING SIDES?

When I started managing people in the 1980s, I bought a book about personnel management. In the chapter on workplace discord, the general message was this: don't take sides. If only it were that simple, right?

When we're resolving a falling-out between two parties, sometimes they ought to meet in the middle and make compromises. Each side needs to give a little. But that's not true all the time. Sometimes people make mistakes and do something wrong. As leaders, we make a judgment call to keep the peace by addressing the wrong and righting it. Taking sides isn't a bad thing, but how we approach the situation makes all the difference. Here are four steps to help you navigate the process:

1. **Listen.** Talk to each person individually and learn their different perspectives. If someone says, "I don't want you to say anything to the other person," stop them. This type of thinking leads to triangulation and away from resolution.
2. **Correct and clarify.** Privately tell each party what needs to change. If a person was wronged, reassure them you're addressing the problem with the other party. If someone made

a mistake, tell them what the consequences will be. At the end of each individual meeting, make your position clear, so there are no surprises.

3. **Resolve.** Bring the parties together and state the resolution. Clarify changes you expect to see when everyone is in the same room at the same time hearing the same message. Employees may not like this, but they'll learn and grow from it.

4. **Coach.** Continue to coach both parties independently so they know they're supported and you're holding them accountable. Now that you're aware of the issue, be observant. Promptly communicate insights and suggestions, so you can help your employees grow and learn.

HOW TO FACILITATE RESOLUTION AFTER CONFLICT

Conflict is inevitable, but combat is optional.[7]

MAX LUCADO

Sometimes, the best way to facilitate reconciliation is to address the friction and then let reconciliation happen naturally. "Kimberly" and "John" were managers in the same department. Kimberly had been with the company for several years and managed programs. John was new and managed people. His casual communication and management styles were the opposite of Kimberly's. She was direct, structured, and energetic. These two skipped the healthy debate stage and went straight to animosity. Any time they worked together, the tension was uncomfortable for other employees.

"Paul," their director, noticed and fielded complaints about what was happening. He confronted them separately and then together. Neither manager could provide any logical reasoning to support their behavior. When they all met, Paul told Kimberly and John they would be taking a mini course that teaches skills to help people work through disagreements with positive results. Paul also clarified that getting along and working well together were job requirements. The two managers had a choice: they could invest energy in arguing with one another, which would lead to a negative outcome for both of them—or they could invest energy in learning how to communicate and work together, which they would both benefit from.

> When we act quickly, we become part of the solution. When we ignore situations, we escalate them.

Paul observed the managers as they went through the course and talked with them about what they were learning. In the meantime, the buzz died down about the two personality clashes, and Paul observed a difference in John's and Kimberly's interactions. While Paul knew the two would never be friends, he still saw professional trust develop between them. They respected each other's differences and produced positive results when working together. In this situation, Paul left the reconciliation to the parties involved, and it worked. They took the course together, but other than that, he didn't force them to become friends or change their personalities.

If a dispute doesn't leave room for reconciliation to happen naturally, here are tips to help employees rebound:

1. Help teams realize the difference between healthy discord and unhealthy friction. If they tiptoe around one another, people become afraid to express differences. Affirm the value of differing viewpoints and point out examples of healthy disagreements.

2. Recognize that after a dispute is resolved, both parties need time and space to recover. If a person privately says, "I still feel upset," or "I'm not sure I trust this person yet," reassure them that this is normal. Encourage employees to give

themselves and the other person time to heal.

3. Don't force people to embrace an unrealistic version of reconciliation. They don't have to be friends; they just have to work together as part of a larger community.

4. Remind employees that they don't have to change their personalities, but they do have to change their professional interactions. People get defensive when they feel they're being asked to change who they are. Reconciliation is easier when they come away with the common goal of changing to improve their work relationship.

IMPORTANT TAKEAWAYS

When we as leaders don't deal with divisive situations, people see us as lacking confidence, competence, and character. But when we successfully navigate people through disputes, we build resilience, rapport, and respect. Every combative situation begins as a tiny disturbance, so *how* and *when* we respond will shape the outcome. When we act quickly, we become part of the solution. When we ignore situations, we escalate them.

CONFLICT RESOLUTION GUIDELINE

DON'T	DO
Skirt the issue	Directly address it
Overreact	Remain calm
Send mixed messages	Clearly state the issue and what must change
Address the conflict unprepared	Keep your message brief and focus on a solution
Assume you'll only address the issue once	Be prepared to follow through if it surfaces again

SACRED WORK

"You must not hate your fellow citizen in your heart. If your neighbor does something wrong, tell him about it, or you will be partly to blame."

LEVITICUS 19:17 NCV[8]

How could the Old Testament, especially the book of Leviticus, possibly apply to managing conflict in today's workplace? It's easy to overlook Leviticus because we see list after list of laws that don't apply to us. Every verse seems to highlight a practice that is painfully irrelevant to us today. As a case in point, Leviticus 11:13–19 lists many birds the Israelites are forbidden from eating, including six different kinds of owls!

But when we look at the big picture of Leviticus, we see this book is less about rules and regulations and more about holy living. All the rules and regulations provided a way for people to recognize a distinctly different God through His distinctly different followers. What better time to step toward holiness than in the middle of a dispute?

Leviticus 19:17 makes it clear that when we ignore wrongdoing, we take ownership of that wrongdoing. The King James Version uses the word *rebuke* in its translation: "Thou shalt not hate thy brother in thine heart: thou shalt in any wise rebuke thy neighbour, and not suffer sin upon him." In Hebrew, the word *rebuke* carries with it the idea of reasoning, correcting, and convincing,[9] all of which are part of successful conflict resolution. Disagreements tend to bring out the worst in people, which is why resolving them presents an incredible opportunity to align our leadership practices with God's standards for holiness.

In this hard stuff of practical holiness, we are not alone. I often say that the Holy Spirit is the most underused superpower that Christians have. Because of the Spirit, we can manage contention using behaviors that reflect holiness. Pray for discernment, courage, and timing. Pray for the people involved and then lead them courageously through it.

My prayer for you: Thank You, Father, for the gift of the Holy Spirit. I pray for the leader reading these words. As she works to transform conflict into peace and wrongs into rights, she'll be in the spotlight. Her employees will notice how she treats each party and what she does to resolve their conflicts. This pressure can shake us as leaders, but I pray she would be reassured by the presence of Your Spirit. Help her to promote peace, as much as she can. Help her make fair decisions and to choose the best way—the holiest way—to resolve whatever strife she is facing. Thank You for what You're going to do as You work through her leadership to strengthen the workplace and everyone involved.

4

Leading Remotely

This change in working arrangements is impossible to overhype.
As big as it is, it's even bigger than people think.[1]

MARC CENEDELLA, CEO, LADDERS

Before *hybrid* and *remote* became commonplace, the company
I worked for was experimenting with the ideas behind the
words. Back then, we lumped everything together and called it "telecommuting." In the early 2000s, these were novel ideas, so employees
had low expectations. The company was dabbling in an area workers
had no experience with but were curious about. They were grateful
we wanted to explore uncharted territory in ways that improved their
quality of life.

At first, people could telecommute if a child was sick, or a home
repair was scheduled during one of those ridiculous four-hour
windows. Salaried employees suggested this policy because they
couldn't spare time away from work, and they wanted to save their
vacation hours for vacations. Personal time off didn't exist. Though
we weren't a dot-com business, we initially felt like one. We'd moved
the company from Georgia to Utah and were struggling to deal with
exponential growth. So we continued to offer telecommuting on a
case-by-case basis.

A couple of years later, a high-performing manager relocated to a different state, and the leadership team voted in favor of having our first fully remote employee. Later, we expanded telecommuting to include workers who were recovering from minor surgeries and new parents who needed time to sort out schedules or childcare. We had a marvelous freedom to create and adapt rules as we went. Perhaps you have nostalgic memories that are similar.

Near the end of my corporate career, people who had been with the company for a minimum of one year could apply to work remotely twice a week. This perk was only available to workers with desk jobs who had a stellar performance history. We offered this option because very few individuals lived in the city where the company was located. Salt Lake City was much more appealing but quite a distance away, so the option to telecommute regularly helped us attract and keep talent.

Though the timeline I've described goes back twenty years, what hindered or set these work models up for success and failure then is remarkably similar to now. What was important decades ago is even more important now: leadership, trust, communication, relationships, and technology. The option to work remotely is no longer a perk; it's the norm. Studies show that in 2023, 27 percent of US employees worked from home.[2] Virtual work began out of necessity with COVID-19, but employees overwhelmingly prefer virtual or hybrid work over being in the office.[3] As with most notable changes, remote work solves some problems and creates others. Current quandaries include:

- How can workers maintain relationships when they rarely see each other face-to-face?
- How often should employees and managers communicate, and what tools are the best?

- Should leaders of blended teams work in-office, from home, or a mix of each?

Everyone is dealing with a radically changed workspace, which has given rise to new work and life stressors. Leaders have to be agile, creative, and intentional as they adapt strategies to set people up for success.

TRANSITIONING TO REMOTE OR HYBRID LEADERSHIP

Maybe you're switching from in-person leadership to remote, or you're transitioning into leading a blended team. Either change is significant. The first step is to accept that work will continue to evolve, but it won't go backward. In-office work will never be the status quo again. The next step is to shift your perspective. *Where* employees work has changed, but *how* they work can now change too. If you hyper fixate on location, you'll miss out on the potential to innovate work at a higher level. Instead of looking at this new way of working as a forced change, what if you started seeing it as an opportunity to redefine what employees do and how they do it?

Here are four steps to help you get started:

1. **Do a solo one-hour brain dump.** Set aside time to get all the ideas, worries, and stressors about teleworking out of your head and onto paper. For the first thirty minutes, focus on the workplace as it existed before. Spend the next thirty minutes focusing on the workplace now. During each half-hour, document and prioritize employee, customer, and business goals. Write about what worked well before and what's working well now. Note what failed or needs improvement. Study the old and new work models to evaluate patterns and make comparisons.

2. **Ask employees what they think about the new way of working.** Don't assume you understand how the work model affects your direct reports. They need the chance to voice observations, ideas, and opinions, and you need their feedback. Invite them into the conversation to promote collaboration and bolster communication. Ask pivotal questions: What about hybrid or off-site has worked well, and what has been a struggle? What are your biggest concerns? What do you need to achieve your goals? What would increase your job satisfaction? What's missing in the work/life balance arena?

3. **Compare your ideas and concerns with those shared by employees.** What are the gaps between the two? Identify pertinent ones and work to repair the disconnect. These gaps help you filter your assumptions through the reality of what workers face. For example, you may regard your company's real-time communication app as wonderful. People can chat instantaneously, no matter if they're at home or in the office. However, if most employees say the app is more of a distraction than a help, you need to change how it's used.

4. **Combine your ideas with employee feedback to outline a prioritized plan.** Steps 1–3 above help you identify the positives and negatives of your company's virtual or blended work structure. Use what you've learned to prioritize what's most important to workers and most critical to the business. Collaborate with your direct reports to set the priority and develop action plans.

BUILDING A REMOTE OR HYBRID WORKPLACE CULTURE

Think of workplace culture as the central nervous system of a company. This system affects how workers feel about the organization, their jobs, customers, and each other. Feelings translate into attitudes and behaviors that impact employee retention, performance, and engagement. Even if your company had a strong culture when traditional offices were the norm, it will need rebuilding in a virtual or hybrid structure.

Some parts of the old ethos can be repurposed, but because the shift to mobile work is drastic, expect the new culture to be markedly different. You can proactively take part in the process, or you can get dragged along while it happens haphazardly.

Passive leaders who see a positive workplace environment more as a perk than a necessity will inevitably deal with high turnover and low employee satisfaction. Underestimating the workplace climate as a primary driver of success is a critical mistake. In a survey by McKinsey & Company of over a thousand companies and three million people, the companies ranking high in work culture also boasted a 60 percent higher return than companies scoring low.[4]

Here are some tips to help you build a new culture as you transition from in-office to digital or blended workspaces:

Maintain your one-on-one meetings but make a few adjustments. Employees whose leaders disappear tend to disappear too. Make sure your direct reports know you're not quiet quitting[5] on them. Doing the minimum work possible is not an option for leaders, and perception is a powerful lens. People need the reassurance of trust and presence, which is built by you.

Consistent check-ins are crucial links between you and the people you lead. If you previously held monthly one-on-ones, shorten the length of the meetings and increase the frequency. By preserving these meetings and having them more often, you let people know they are your highest priority. You're also preempting the negative impact that may happen from a lack of in-person interaction.

Make sure logistical arrangements consider the practical needs of the business but also the personal needs of the employee. For example, digital workers value flexibility and often need it to manage other responsibilities. Don't require employees to use video; make it optional. Researchers at Stanford have validated how video chats cause fatigue.[6] Videoconferencing shouldn't be banned, but as Stanford Professor Jeremy Bailenson points out, "just because you *can* use video doesn't mean you *have* to."[7]

> Being present is one of the most valuable gifts leaders can give their direct reports. Because you aren't in the office with them, being attentive during calls and video chats is key.

Most importantly, listen. Being present is one of the most valuable gifts leaders can give their direct reports. Because you aren't in the office with them, being attentive during calls and video chats is key. Notice what workers are saying or not saying. Are they stressed and disengaged, or passionate and excited? What needs do they have? What do they love about their work? What's frustrating them? Take notes during check-ins and process what you've written later. Develop plans to support and serve people based on these conversations.

Create strong, engaging teams. Because of the Great Resignation[8] and other factors, there's a chance the team you're leading never worked side by side at all in the office. Collaboration is difficult without connection, and connection doesn't happen by coincidence. Your responsibility is to create cohesiveness.

Establish clear guardrails for on-site and off-site workers. Once you create ground rules, they won't have to wonder how communication and scheduling will work. Protocols eliminate confusion and prevent division between in-person and digital employees. At the onset, include direct reports in brainstorming sessions about communication parameters. Discuss how flexible schedules will be managed and communicated and how collaborative meetings will be handled. Clarify that prompt, honest feedback is valuable and needed.

Ultimately, you'll make the final decisions on what the rules are and how to enforce them. Your goal isn't to micromanage, but to establish boundaries, so employees know what to expect from one another. Set the expectation that new work models will change a few times before they settle.

Consistently meet as a team by phone or video. Keep these meetings short and don't limit them to work topics. When you give people time to get to know one another, you send the message that relationships are important, and this message becomes part of the company culture. Likewise, provide opportunities for the team to meet in person, even if it's once a quarter or once a year. Where workers live will affect the frequency, but don't let logistics become an obstacle. Culture requires an investment of time, intention, energy, and money. Plan ahead and budget accordingly.

Make sure everyone knows what goals teams are working toward and why. Individual goals increase engagement, and collective goals increase unity. If everyone understands how goals contribute to the well-being of the team and the company, they develop a sense of purpose, which motivates employees to work—and to work together.

Be mindful about expressing gratitude to remote workers. When you work on-site, you naturally have regular and consistent interactions with your direct reports. You buy them coffee or lunch because proximity makes it easy. Distance workers miss out on words and gestures of appreciation that happen in an office environment. Don't stop seeing and valuing people who work from home just because they're not in-office regularly. These suggestions will help:

- Praise employees in front of others. Do this during video meetings or in group or company emails.
- Send handwritten notes and cards. It doesn't matter if someone lives five minutes away or in another state, handwritten expressions of thanks are powerful.
- Use gifts or gift cards. You don't need to spend a lot of money to show you value your team. Send a gift card to a favorite coffee shop or restaurant or use a food delivery service to surprise them with lunch.
- Send a recorded message or video voicemail. This is a great option when you want to express thanks for a specific achievement. A prerecorded message or video is a noninvasive way to thank and recognize them.
- Tailor your gratitude to fit each employee's preferences. Whether in-office or virtual, workers are unique in how they prefer to receive appreciation. What resonates with one may be off-putting to another. As you get to know them, note their preferences.

PREVENTING INEQUITY IN HYBRID MODELS

Studies by the Society of Human Resource Management show that managers and leaders in hybrid work models suffer from proximity bias,[9] meaning they're more attentive to in-office employees than those who work from home. Essentially, out of sight equals out of mind.[10] Bias leads to negative assumptions, micromanagement, and inequitable treatment. Leaders can't afford for this bias to become the norm. Here's a list of nine safeguards to help you prevent inequity from happening in a blended work environment:

1. Take it seriously if remote workers mention concerns about inequity. Provide a safe space for them to talk about how they're impacted by bias. Document their concerns and ask questions to learn more. Do they think remote work is pushing their contributions into the background? Do they feel they're missing opportunities because they're not on-site? Ask for specific examples so you can create a plan to mitigate these vulnerabilities.

2. Reevaluate how you evaluate. Review all performance measurements to ensure they emphasize results and output. If measurements depend on or are influenced by time spent in the office, change the measurements. Is the performance criteria in line with what people can realistically achieve? Are performance evaluations standardized to protect against bias?

3. Build trust to manage accountability. Don't rely on surveillance systems; they represent the opposite of trust and have the opposite effect. These systems create unnecessary burdens on your teams and set you up as a micromanager. Instead, empower people to solve problems and make decisions on their own. Giving them authority and autonomy builds trust and boosts productivity. Employees will own their work and their results.

4. Consider the impact of your own work structure. If you choose to work on-site every day, you could be contributing to bias. Think about working remotely on a regular basis. Doing this counteracts the idea that only employees who work in person daily are effective and valuable. Spend equal time working from home and at the office.

5. When you choose to have video meetings, require everyone to attend by video, even if some participants are on-site. This equalizes the experience for all team members.

6. If you're on-site and you notice team members working together in a way that excludes other members who are off-site, call it out. Prompt them to include the off-site team member.

7. Publicly talk about how biases against remote workers can creep into the workplace.

8. Immediately dismantle words and actions that create an "us against them" mentality.

9. Participate in and provide bias training for all your direct reports. It's imperative that employees who work remotely, have young children at home, or have flex schedules aren't viewed as poor performers. In many cases, these workers will be women. As leaders, it's our responsibility to bridge the gap between assumptions and reality, and outside training helps.

SACRED WORK

All Scripture is God-breathed and is useful for teaching, rebuking, correcting and training in righteousness, so that the servant of God may be thoroughly equipped for every good work.

2 TIMOTHY 3:16–17

We think of Scripture as teaching broader concepts like love, truth, and kindness. But if we look closely, we can connect biblical teaching to the present day in surprising ways. For example, in 2 Timothy 3:17, the word *work* in the original Greek means "to toil (as an effort or occupation)."[11] Here, the word *work* means now what it meant then. God cares about our work: what we do, how we do it, and the problems we face. His Word teaches and equips us in timely, relevant ways. There's even an application for remote work leadership!

In the book of Acts, we read how the gospel spread from Israel to Judea, Samaria, and the ends of the earth (as told in the book of Acts). At first, kingdom workers clustered in close-knit communities, eating, working, and studying Scripture together as a community. When they helped the poor or preached the gospel, they did it collectively.

After Stephen was martyred, the apostles and other Christ followers were scattered like seeds (Acts 8:1–4). What Christ said would happen in Acts 1:8 began to unfold. People who were used to praying and working together were far apart, doing the same work in different places. They had the same mission but carried it out in different ways. From these early kingdom workers, we learn practical lessons about staying connected, even when we're physically separated.

1. **Prioritize communication.** The early church didn't have the luxury of technology, but they wrote letters—lots of letters. Paul's letters to various churches and individuals make up a chunk of the New Testament.[12] He was consistent, encouraging, and instructionally clear. Unlike letters, digital communication is immediate. But consistency and clarity are still key, and encouragement is still powerful.

2. **Build relationships.** Genuine relationships with virtual employees don't just happen; you have to build them. First-century believers found common ground and were connected by a common purpose. Commonalities bound them together when miles kept them apart. A shared mission and shared priorities connect your team, no matter

how diverse. Personalize these connections by getting to know your team and providing forums for them to learn about each other. People want meaningful work and genuine interactions.

3. **Connect in person when possible.** Instead of planes, the early church traveled on foot, by donkey, or by boat.[13] Even though Paul frequently communicated by letter, he also visited churches and individuals whenever he could. Company policies and employee home bases will affect whether you and your team can meet up. As an alternative, travel to meet with them. You may have to plan several trips to see everyone, but the time and effort are worth the payoff.

4. **Hire trustworthy talent.** Early church leaders couldn't always be physically present with kingdom workers. Paul, for example, enlisted other leaders like Timothy to lead regional churches and gospel efforts (see Acts 19:22). The Holy Spirit (and strong personal references) prompted Paul to choose Timothy. Godly discernment and leadership savvy don't disappear just because work models change. Be prayerful, patient, and thorough in your hiring practices, and trust the people you hire.

5. **Establish traditions.** No matter where they lived, those in the early church prayed daily at 9:00 a.m. and 3:00 p.m.[14] They took comfort in knowing other believers were praying simultaneously in different places. The tradition of set prayer times united them. Similarly, you can establish traditions with your remote teams. Reserve the first five minutes of team meetings for casual conversation. Create programs where workers recognize and reward their peers. Do a monthly shout-out for accomplishments. These simple traditions foster belonging and create unity.

Women who lead remote or blended teams often feel isolated, as if no one can relate to their challenges. Many feel forced to figure out what to do in the moment. In ancient times, godly leaders of faraway teams overcame similar issues. We can apply their timeless lessons to our leadership, knowing the same God who guided them into unfamiliar territory guides us too.

5

Leading Through Crisis

Do not be anxious about anything, but in every situation, by prayer and
petition, with thanksgiving, present your requests to God. And the peace
of God, which transcends all understanding, will guard your hearts and
your minds in Christ Jesus.

PHILIPPIANS 4:6–7

W e've all experienced seasons in our careers that were unfor-
gettable for all the wrong reasons. At some point, leaders will
inevitably square off against a workplace crisis that threatens their
company's stability and deeply affects the people they're responsible for. Crises impact people and organizations to varying degrees.
These situations may involve a personnel issue like a harassment suit,
a financial issue like budget cuts, or an external event like 9/11, the
2007–2008 recession, or COVID-19.

Extreme challenges like these threaten a company's ability to operate its business effectively, and it's our responsibility to navigate
our direct reports in a way that inspires hope and dispels fear. Crisis
management is not a single skill and can't be stripped down to a
simple process or procedure. What weakens a company during an
emergency is unprepared leadership, which leads to unprepared

teams and harmful long-term consequences. Your team's ability to deal with a turbulent situation will, in large part, correlate to how well you've prepared them for one.

Is your team nimble and flexible? Do they know how to collaborate to reach a common goal? Does your culture lend itself to problem-solving and collaboration? Do people feel comfortable voicing obstacles and questions? Are you already known as a leader who brings calm, resilience, and optimism into tough circumstances? These are questions we need to ask ourselves before a catastrophe ever hits, so we can build a work culture that can confront a crisis and thrive through it. When leaders foster teams that excel at crisis management, companies can recover quickly. The company's culture, relationships, and processes come out stronger on the other side.

THE CRISIS OF 9/11

Leadership exists when people are no longer victims of
circumstances but participate in creating new circumstances.[1]

PETER SENGE, MIT SLOAN SCHOOL OF MANAGEMENT

Do you remember what you were doing or where you were working when 9/11 happened? I was a director of operations, and the day started normally for me and my departments on that Tuesday morning, just as it did for companies across the United States. All that changed when news of the terrorist attack was broadcast.

This external event hit our company with waves of shock and fear that continued throughout the day. Employees who had relatives and customers in New York City frantically tried to reach them by phone. Others streamed the news on their PCs. The phones didn't ring, and an eerie silence replaced the normal daily hubbub throughout our building.

Our company's leadership immediately accepted that this tragic day would not be productive. My first business mentor, Steve Hudson, told me, "If you take care of your employees, they'll take care of everything else." I've found this to be true in most situations, especially a crisis. After a brief meeting, our leadership team took the following steps:

1. We gathered everyone together, acknowledged what was going on, and gave them the opportunity to voice their concerns. Concerns were addressed or tabled, depending on the urgency. For example, if workers were worried about their families and wanted to go home, we told them to go home. If someone wanted to know how business travel would be handled in the coming months, we parked the question and said we'd circle back to it. We communicated our plan for the day and committed to another brief stand-up meeting the next morning.

2. Workers who remained in the building were encouraged to stay in contact with their loved ones throughout the day. When adversity hits, employees are calmer if they know that what they value is safe. With 9/11, most people were concerned about their friends or families.

3. Our IT department set up viewing stations in a few key areas throughout the company, so people could be together while keeping up to date on what was happening in the news.

4. Our HR manager reminded workers of the employee assistance program, which offered free counseling.

5. Managers organized staffing so departments took turns covering for one another. This made it possible for employees to go home, make calls, or catch up on the news without interrupting business.

6. Leaders helped take care of customers, whether that meant answering phones and emails or shipping products.

In the immediate aftermath, workers took the lead in organizing cash and equipment donations to help rescue efforts. Our company manufactured rescue equipment, so we contributed headlamps and gear. The donation project gave us all something positive to focus on. In the days, weeks, and months that followed, we continued an open dialogue about 9/11 and how it was affecting our lives and the business. In morning standups, individuals voiced unease about air travel safety and the economy. We let them know we had the same concerns and were closely watching market reactions and the buying habits of our customers. We also told them we were cutting air travel for the immediate future.

Gradually, meetings became more infrequent, and everyone shifted their focus from the event to helping solve challenges resulting from it. The customer service and sales departments collected and relayed customer feedback, so we could better assess the business climate. Managers were mindful of being consistent with their one-on-one meetings, so employees who didn't feel comfortable sharing in a group could share privately.

Our sales numbers held steady in the months after 9/11, but we decided to be extremely conservative with air travel. In 2001, videoconferencing wasn't a standard practice and our owner lived abroad, so decisions to cut travel weren't made lightly. We held brainstorming sessions about how to prioritize travel and what to do in place of trade shows and other meetings already on the calendar. An important national sales meeting was canceled, and instead, our external sales representatives held regional meetings clients could drive to. A frontline employee made this suggestion in one of our morning standups, and it offered a brilliant solution that sales reps and clients both appreciated.

Six months after 9/11, we asked workers to help us assess how we'd managed the crisis. We were surprised to learn they appreciated what we *didn't* do as much as what we did. Here are a few of the things we didn't do:

overreact or underreact

prioritize sales over people

view company gatherings as a waste of time

treat salaried and hourly workers differently

set hard and fast dates for when the new way of working would end

talk more than we listened

expect everyone to respond to 9/11 in the same way

THE PANDEMIC

Fast forward to 2019. COVID-19 struck eighteen years after 9/11, and it was arguably a vastly different predicament: the pandemic was global and negatively impacted the health and lives of people and workplaces around the world. I'm sure you were affected too. Single parents, primarily women, homeschooled their children while working from home. Two-parent families had to sort out where home offices would be and what it looked like to have their children literally in the workspace with them.

Leaders scrambled to establish secure and efficient off-site workstations for their teams, while simultaneously plunging into remote leadership. Distribution and retail environments were outfitted with plexiglass and six-foot quadrants, and new safety protocols were implemented. Medical care workers who reported to the frontline faced exposure to the virus and potentially bringing it home to their families.

Restaurants shifted their efforts to pickup and delivery—and when that wasn't an option, many restaurants were forced to close. The same held true for service providers that weren't considered essential. Millions of people lost their jobs; e-commerce boomed while in-person retail shopping ground to a halt. McKinsey Global Institute reported in February 2021 that about 25 percent of workers were forced to change careers because of the pandemic.[2]

Companies poured efforts into creating new sustainable work environments, as they tried to stabilize business amid challenges and change. The three main areas where leadership struggled were in their immediate reactions, overall communication, and addressing the impact of COVID-19 on working women.

Imbalanced reactions: Early in the pandemic, individuals shared stories with me about sales managers who were forced to attend large, crowded events with potential clients in locations where the six-foot rule wasn't enforced. Other workers told me they felt forced to be in close contact with customers or their jobs would be jeopardized. Their bosses acted as if the COVID environment didn't exist. On the other end of the spectrum, an individual who worked in a large distribution center told me safety protocols changed multiple times a week with meager communication or apparent direction.

One director shared how her CEO implemented a hybrid environment because he wanted employees and departments to reconnect in person for better synergy. In order to maintain state safety requirements, desks were moved and barricaded, and elaborate office schedules were developed, so only a few people were in the office at a time. The result? Not exactly the synergistic connection that was intended. This is a great example of good intentions but poor results.

Communication: Corporations found that remote work reduced costs because it eliminated a chunk of overhead. As a result, many have decided to have employees work remotely indefinitely.[3] I coach several leaders who say that before decisions about work models were finalized, they provided short, monthly updates to their direct reports about the status of remote work. Even when leaders weren't 100 percent sure what would happen next, they recognized how remote work affected their teams and used emails to encourage dialogue.

If the scale tipped in favor of permanent remote work, these leaders communicated what might be on the horizon. They also solicited feedback from employees. For example, many individuals loved eliminating their commute time and expense, but others wanted to return to the office. They struggled to conduct business at home with their families present, or they missed the creative energy of working in person with other people.

Even though officials declared the pandemic over in 2023, some companies remain undecided about what the new normal will be, so their employees keep treading water, waiting for decisions.[4] Because they don't receive consistent communication themselves, many leaders tell me they don't know what to tell workers. Others say they receive updates about what the future workplace will look like at the same time their staff does. Leaders can't weigh in or think through logistics or the impact on their teams. Regardless of whether a workplace remains a remote environment, moves back to the office, or becomes a hybrid of both, employee satisfaction correlates with how well (or poorly) leadership communicates in the time frame leading up to the decision.

Women and COVID-19: Before COVID-19, the number of professional women was on the upswing as women filled more and more leadership positions. During the pandemic, however, the trend went in the opposite direction. Working moms, women in senior leadership positions, and women of color all considered leaving the workforce or downshifting positions to decrease work and life stresses.[5] Whether as single or dual parents, studies show women carry the bulk of household and family responsibilities in addition to their jobs.[6]

Companies that recognized these vulnerabilities and chose to invest in women allowed for flexible work-from-home schedules and focused on results rather than forcing everyone into the same remote policies. Attentive leaders actively communicated with women professionals and recognized how they were impacted differently from their counterparts. They accepted the aftermath of COVID-19 as the reality. Even today, organizations that honor women professionals understand that the challenges women face are unique, so they build policies and work cultures intent on helping women stay in the labor force.

Other organizations failed to dig into the diverse issues professional women are facing. There is often a frantic push by leaders to return to a pre-pandemic environment, and it seems easier to standardize schedules and policies than to customize them. These companies keep hammering goals and initiatives without prioritization or consideration for how the business landscape has changed and how individuals now need more flexibility to manage life and work.

As I've interacted with women leaders across the country, I've found that the same basic guardrails that helped my leadership team navigate 9/11 can apply to any crisis:

BASIC LEADERSHIP GUARDRAILS FOR CRISIS MANAGEMENT

DO	DON'T
Be transparent and engage workers in finding solutions.	Overlook people because other parts of the business seem more important or easier to manage.
Create ways for teams to share their concerns, questions, and ideas.	Dominate the narrative.
Strive for balance.	Overreact or underreact.
Align the frequency and method of communication based on how significantly a change or decision will impact individuals.	Underestimate the need for consistent communication.
Make timely decisions that keep the business moving but in a way that allows space for change.	Make permanent and hasty decisions in an unpredictable, changing environment.
Keep a pulse on what workers need so they can continue to contribute to the health of the company.	Overlook the diversity of what workers need to thrive in the aftereffects.

IMPORTANT TAKEAWAYS

Emergency situations catch everyone off guard and bring risk into the organization. It's vital that leaders quickly acknowledge the situation for what it is and then act. All crises require action, and we must use our authority and resources to navigate our teams through it. The longer we wait to lead, the more our employees will remain fearful and unfocused.

Leaders will feel apprehensive naturally, but we have to move past our personal feelings so we can create solutions. Our core responsibilities don't change when we're faced with calamity. If we're confident in our roles and responsibilities, we'll automatically defer to them when a crisis hits. To instill calm, we have to remain calm and lead people from one situation to the next until the trouble subsides. This strategy creates order in chaos and instills hope in our teams.

Expect predicaments to reveal weak spots within organizations, teams, and leaders. Acknowledge the weak spots and collaborate with your teams on problem-solving. When we trust our employees to engage in their own outcomes, we create opportunities for them to come out of a crisis stronger than when they went in.

SACRED WORK

Then Esther sent this reply to Mordecai: "Go, gather together all the Jews who are in Susa, and fast for me. Do not eat or drink for three days, night or day. I and my attendants will fast as you do. When this is done, I will go to the king, even though it is against the law. And if I perish, I perish."

ESTHER 4:15–16

Just as Esther's Jewish identity didn't change when she became the queen of a Persian empire, our identity as Christians doesn't change when we become leaders. When confronted with a crisis, we're able to stand on the foundation of our faith as an added support and source of encouragement. The story of Esther models the sound leadership principles we've looked at. When faced with an urgent crisis, she

acted quickly,
communicated well and often,

strategically made requests,

enlisted help from others,

put her people first, and

united them toward a common goal.

Esther's leadership and God's intervention kept the Jewish people from being destroyed. We don't face that level of threat as we lead in the workplace, but we can still apply biblical leadership principles to help us lead our teams through modern-day crises. We can believe that God purposefully placed us in leadership roles as stewards of the people He has entrusted us with. He would never give us that responsibility without equipping us to follow through with it.

My prayer for you: Father, I lift up to You the leader who is reading this. I pray You would breathe unquenchable hope into her heart, her spirit, and her leadership. Fix her eyes on You, the One who is greater than any trial we face on earth. Help her steer her team through this crisis in a way that inspires hope and dispels fear. Thank You for her faithfulness to You and for being her anchor in this storm.

6

Leading Through Change

Any time there is change, there is opportunity. So it is paramount that an organization get energized rather than paralyzed.[1]

JOHN C. MAXWELL

When it comes to change, I'm split down the middle. At work, I welcome it because I've learned that change usually results in something better. But in my personal life? No, thank you. In my home life, consistency equals comfort. I like structure and routine, and I dislike big upheavals—like moving.

My husband, George, and I met in our forties, and because God has a sense of humor, we've moved five times over the past decade. We're building what we hope will be our last home, and I'm grateful it's only five miles from where we live now. This will be the easiest move ever! But because we still need to sell our old house, we've been forced to adopt a new routine:

Spot clean and do a walk-through every morning.

Put everything in its place throughout the day, every day.

Prepare to grab the dog and leave at any moment.

Prepare to have your work interrupted. And then interrupted again.

We altered our habits almost overnight. The disruptions and checklists are a hassle, but we're motivated because we understand why they're important, and we see the potential result on the other side. I share this tidbit from my personal life because it translates to work; when we're leading through transitions in the workplace, our employees want and deserve the same understanding. For change to succeed, they need to understand the "why" and the possibilities.

GUIDING PRINCIPLES

Years of experience have taught me that new systems, processes, and buildings come with grand improvements. I'm all for it. But not everyone has had the same experiences I have. Workers who are new to a company, industry, or the workforce may be more averse to change. The same is true of employees who remember mishandled upheavals and the fallout. With careful planning, leaders can increase the chances of successful change management and decrease employee concerns, but this isn't always possible.

Forced change doesn't allow for careful planning and compels leaders to pilot through decisions outside their control. These situations include scenarios that may be familiar to you: external crises, leadership turnover, and changes in human resources policies or federal regulations. Because unplanned shifts are chaotic, success leans heavily on the strength of the organization and its leaders.

Amy Lively, leader and co-owner of The Lively Merchant, says, "It's important to have smart business practices, a strong work culture, and solid relationships in place before an unplanned change hits. Unexpected changes age your organization faster than normal circumstances. The outcomes can be positive or negative."[2]

This idea ties to Matthew 7:24–27:

> "Everyone who hears these words of mine and puts them into practice is like a wise man who built his house on the rock. The rain came down, the streams rose, and the winds blew and beat against that house; yet it did not fall, because it had its foundation on the rock. But everyone who hears these words of mine and does not put them into practice is like a foolish man who built his house on sand. The rain came down, the streams rose, and the winds blew and beat against that house, and it fell with a great crash."

In these verses, the rock's foundation represents obedience to Jesus' teachings, but the metaphor applies to other things in life too. Scripture gives us both soulful and sensible advice. As Amy says, "You can't look outside, see the storm, and then scramble to build a strong foundation. You need to have one already in place."[3] If your work infrastructure is weak, employees won't withstand abrupt shifts without a negative impact. However, a solid base provides them with stability and confidence when your company is jarred by unavoidable change.

It's better to slow the process than to speed the failure.

Whether a change is planned or unplanned, positive or negative, human nature is to resist. McKinsey & Company did a study showing that 70 percent of initiated change in the workplace doesn't achieve the outcomes leaders wanted, and worker resistance was the number one reason.[4] So how can you initiate transitions in a way that engages people instead of turning them away? How will you minimize the impact? What can you do to secure successful outcomes during times of change?

Here are four guiding principles:

1. **Identify and bridge the perspective gap.** Leaders and employees almost always have two different perspectives on change. To maximize the chances of success, you need to bridge the gap between the two. Empathy helps! I know how uncomfortable I feel when going through personal shake-ups, so I relate to how workers feel about professional ones. If you know what workers think and feel, you're able to meet them where they are. Once you understand their perspective, you can move on to address their concerns and questions.

2. **Communicate early and often.** The more impactful the change, the more important the communication. Very few people like surprises that disrupt their workspace. If employees are invited to learn about new locations, policies, or systems in the idea stage, they'll be much more likely to warm up to the possibilities.

   Consider issuing small updates during team or departmental meetings, so when the idea becomes a decision, it won't be a surprise. Some leaders hesitate to do this because they worry the change won't actually materialize. But if it doesn't happen, people will understand, and most will be glad they were in the loop. Proactive communication establishes trust.

3. **Dismantle resistance by dismantling fear.** Employees resist transitions when they think something valuable is being replaced with something less-than. The best way to dismantle the resistance is to dismantle the fear. First, pay attention to learn what they're afraid of. What are their concerns? What questions are they asking? Do they understand what's happening and how it will impact them? Are they leaning into worst-case scenarios?

After you learn what's feeding their fears, counteract the fear with facts and reassurances. Workers may raise concerns you don't have answers for. Be honest and document their concerns so you can follow up when you have more information.

4. **Pay attention to red flags and adjust accordingly.** If a shift is in process and red flags are raised, stop the ship and correct the course. It's better to slow the process than to speed the failure. Your role as a leader includes understanding the difference between progressive discord and warning bells. When organizations restructure departments, implement new programs, or re-engineer procedures, individuals won't always agree. Decisions and next steps need healthy debates to keep pushing them forward.

On the other hand, if you're pushing a timeline and teams are consistently pushing back, that's a red flag. If a planning session results in the discovery of a giant legal or financial obstacle, that's a red flag. These types of warnings don't require you to stop change from happening, but you do need to adjust. You may need to slow the timeline, add resources, or pause and regroup.

THE PERSPECTIVE GAP EXPLAINED

The *perspective gap* is a term I created to explain the difference between how leaders and workers view organizational change. When not acknowledged and addressed, this gap creates tremendous frustration for both groups. Leaders decide to rebrand, expand into new markets, or move the company, and they can't contain their excitement. But when workers find out, they're skeptical, suspicious, and worried. These contradictory viewpoints create friction that threatens relationships and progress.

Once we understand *why* these opposing perspectives exist, we can stop them from accelerating in opposite directions.

Leaders have time to process change before their employees do. When you unveil a change to your employees, you've likely known about it for some time. You've processed the risks and the unknowns. Meetings, conversations, and planning sessions with other leaders have already happened. With departmental changes, you may be authorized to communicate with your team ahead of time. But with global switches, such as layoffs, mergers, or shifting from on-site to remote work, leaders aren't allowed to have piecemeal discussions with their departments. Even if you're able to talk to your team in the early stages, they'll still find out about a turn of events after you and other leaders do.

Remember, people need time and support to process what's happening. Before your employees can be excited about the next chapter ahead, they need time to get on the same page.

Anticipate the questions. Before unveiling a change, anticipate the questions your workers will have and prepare answers for them. Going through this process helps you see the change through their eyes. It's impossible to predict every question, but the big hitters are straightforward:

- When?
- What's required of us?
- How will it positively/negatively affect us?
- What are the risks or downsides?
- How long will it last?
- What's in it for us?
- What's the expected outcome?

It's natural for people to ask these questions, and it's important for leaders to think through their answers in advance. If there are big-hitter questions you don't have answers for, you know you need to tighten up your plan. As a change agent, you have to be able to articulate your "why" in a meaningful way because the better your team understands the reason behind a transition, the more motivated they'll be to make it happen. If you're not convinced of the reason, they won't be either.

Leaders embrace change-related risk because they have more security. Frontline employees are less willing to risk because they have more to lose. They make less money, have less job security, and less control over their jobs and the work environment. One recent study of 79,000 workers and leaders showed that C-suite leaders are 66 percent more likely to embrace risks from change management initiatives than other workers.[5] Overall, 40 percent of executives like taking change-related risks.[6] But the number for frontline employees was only 24 percent.[7] Clearly, many workers associate change with risk, while leaders associate change with opportunity. This is another part of the perspective gap, and why we have to find a way to merge differing viewpoints within the organization.

> Imagining yourself in their position reminds you to care about your team's concerns and to be gentle with any resistance they might have.

What you can do: A little empathy goes a long way. You're the sum of your experiences, and the same is true of your team. They don't have your background, work history, or the security of your title and position. Think back to when you started your career. How would you feel if you were suddenly faced with a complete departure from routines and processes you understood and were comfortable with? Imagining yourself in their position, without your current job security, reminds you to care about your team's concerns and to be gentle with any resistance they might have.

You'll also want to create opportunities for teams to explain what seems risky to them, so you can see risks from their viewpoint. Give them ample time to talk through what's bothering them before you jump into problem-solving mode. Ask questions to get a clear understanding and repeat their concerns back, so they know you understood.

When I was a logistics director, we decided to adjust our warehouse layout. Our customers demanded new value-added services like having products ticketed with custom price tags. If we lengthened and restructured the conveyors, our warehouse technicians would spend less time pushing product carts around and instead could use the time working on the new services. During the initial conversation, however, it surprised me to see and hear our team's reluctance about the proposed adjustments.

When we dug deeper, the warehouse manager and I learned the reasons behind their concerns. Apparently, we had placed such an emphasis on the savings in labor hours that the team wondered if the technology would eventually replace them. I empathized with this fear because I remembered what it was like to be an hourly employee trying to make ends meet. Any threat to job security was a threat to a person's livelihood.

Once we understood this concern, we reiterated how the saved labor hours would transfer over from one type of work to another. I showed them a chart of how much more money important customers were spending with us that year and explained that now these customers expected us to meet all their special requirements. There was no automated solution to applying price stickers to each product or special labels to boxes. Technology couldn't solve these tasks, so the new layout would allow us to shift labor hours from picking product to doing value-added services. The explanation eased their worries, but they had another concern.

The team was also nervous about the expense of the warehouse modification because they thought it would eat into their wages. We could see how they would arrive at this conclusion because they weren't responsible for the departmental budget and weren't privy to how it worked. Many of the workers hadn't yet received their annual raises, which added to their worries. The warehouse manager explained that the budget for the project was separate and unrelated to their wages. He reassured them that their pay was intact and raises would carry on as planned.

Our initial meeting to communicate the change ended up taking much longer than anticipated, but the extra time was needed. The warehouse team left the meeting knowing we heard and understood them. We left knowing they were on board with the change because of it.

Employees think of issues the leadership team overlooked. Leaders represent departments or teams made up of individuals who are involved in the daily work at a deeper level. Although leaders are the decision-makers, the individuals impacted by transitions will naturally think of issues that leaders did not. Most leaders are visionaries and concentrate on where the organization needs to go more than on how it will get there. They hire talented people who focus on details, execution, and safeguarding their areas of specialty. So a perspective gap will probably exist between the problems leaders expect and the problems employees expect.

What you can do: To close the gap, you'll want to provide a regular forum for people to voice their concerns and questions and a regular process for resolving them. Your employees will have valuable insights and compelling questions that will ultimately make the transition smoother and have better outcomes. Go into each communication session with a collaborative, curious attitude, and respect their expertise by posturing yourself to listen and learn.

Here are four steps to help you hold effective Q&A sessions with your team:

1. Celebrate the fact that employees have questions and will voice them! Engaged teams are curious and aren't afraid to speak up.
2. Give them the opportunity to ask questions and make it safe for them to do so. This means listening without dismissing concerns and without interrupting.
3. Park questions that can't be answered during the meeting. Answers may have to wait because you don't have them or because of time constraints. If you don't know an answer, admit that—then follow up promptly.
4. Be transparent. Keep the unanswered questions in a place accessible to all workers. This creates accountability for leaders and shows a resolution path everyone can follow.

SACRED WORK

I love that God graciously provides us with change agents and fresh-start moments to give us hope and help us believe that change is possible and can be successful. Throughout the Old Testament, we see judges, kings, and prophets who worked tirelessly on God's behalf to turn desperate situations around for the better. After the book of Malachi, we have a little white space of four hundred years[8] before the most powerful change agent of all makes an entry: Jesus.

When Jesus arrives on the scene in the first-century Jewish world, religious leaders had the ultimate say about who was or wasn't a sinner. There were volumes of rules designed to keep the worthy in and the unworthy out. Jesus turned these rules upside down by giving everyone access to God. Cultural and social customs were upended by grace.

The Samaritan woman Jesus met at the well was an outcast (see John 4). There were high walls between her and Jesus. He was Jewish, a man, and a rabbi—and according to cultural and religious norms should have avoided traveling through Samaria and talking to this woman at all costs. But not our changemaker. There He is in the noonday heat, asking her for a drink. Tradition was that if Jesus were to drink from a water jar touched by a Samaritan, He would become ceremonially unclean.[9] The Samaritan woman is startled and maybe even skeptical. "The Samaritan woman said to him, 'You are a Jew and I am a Samaritan woman. How can you ask me for a drink?' (For Jews do not associate with Samaritans)" (John 4:9).

I understand her skepticism. If we hear a message about ourselves often enough, we begin to believe it's true. If perfectionism and keeping the rules seem more important than relationship, we're tempted to fall behind in both. When someone comes along and edits these narratives, we naturally step back with arms crossed and brows furrowed. Jesus understands this now, just as He did thousands of years ago. His compassion and empathy are timeless.

As the conversation between Jesus and the woman continues, it becomes theological (see John 4:10–26). The Samaritans worshiped the true God, but they didn't worship in truth: their Bible only contained the first five books, and they didn't accept God's revelation beyond that.[10] Jesus states the Messiah will come from God's historic people and explains that worship requires more than conforming to rituals performed in a certain place; it requires the right inward spirit or heart attitude. Samaritans knew little about the Messiah, though they did anticipate His coming. They thought of the Messiah more as a teacher, and she thinks that when this teacher comes, he would clarify what she and Jesus are talking about.

Next comes my favorite part of the story. "Then Jesus declared, 'I, the one speaking to you—I am he'" (John 4:26). What just happened?! The woman at the well, shamed and shunned, became the first person to hear that Jesus was the Messiah. The same woman who normally hid from the community, doing everything she could to avoid others, immediately went into town and shared what happened to her. She was so overcome that she left her water jar behind. Despite her reputation, the woman's story was compelling, and the townspeople were so impressed they came to see Jesus for themselves.

Jesus gave the woman at the well respect, compassion, and empathy. He told her the truth about who He was and who she could be in Him. All these fresh-start moments became dots connected on a road map to something better—something so much better that it drew a crowd back to the source, Jesus, a disruptor of the very best kind. From Him, we understand that even the most welcome change may be met with fear and suspicion. From Him, we understand how gaps between people can be bridged with respect, compassion, empathy, and truth.

Be respectful, and the people you lead will trust you.

Be compassionate, and they'll take heart.

Be empathetic, and they'll know you see them.

Be truthful, and the changed will become the changemakers.

7

Leading in a Male-Dominated Industry

For we are God's handiwork, created in Christ Jesus to do good
works, which God prepared in advance for us to do.

EPHESIANS 2:10

God designed men and women differently, but He values us
equally. In the Bible, we read about women leading in spaces
where they're in the minority. Think about Deborah, Esther, Lydia,
and Phoebe.[1] All these women accomplished important work for
God's kingdom.

I spent most of my career in industries where women were the
minority. This type of workspace can be difficult. But it also uniquely
positions you to advocate for other women. Helping women succeed
doesn't mean you don't want men to succeed. It means you want
everyone to succeed, and you'll do what it takes to make that happen.

My mentor, Catherine Gates, often talks about how men and
women can maximize their potential together as leaders. In her
book *The Confidence Cornerstone* she writes, "Men and women
were designed to work together. When we each use the unique gifts
God blessed us with collaboratively, we can do great things. When
we compete with one another . . . when we put each other down, we

create division where unity was intended. We diminish what's possible and damage what God designed."[2]

When we see greater-than and lesser-than signs in the workplace, God didn't create those, we did. As godly leaders (men and women), we're responsible for addressing and correcting these inequities and doing so with love.

WOMEN WHO LEAD IN MALE-DOMINATED SPACES

Many companies and industries today embrace women leaders, but corporate America still has a long way to go. There are still industries where women fight to progress into leadership positions or to overcome constraints or unequal treatment. McKinsey & Company found that out of six hundred companies, women in leadership positions are trending upward, but they represent less than half of leadership positions.[3] Sometimes, the number dropped below 25 percent. For every one hundred men promoted to manager, only eighty-five women were promoted.[4] Industries with 25 percent or fewer women are classified as male-dominated,[5] and these industries tend to foster inequitable work environments that make it difficult for women to succeed:

Top Ten Male-Dominated Industries[6]

Agriculture

Architecture

Construction

Engineering

Finance

Information technology and software development

Manufacturing

Mining, quarrying, oil, and gas

Science

Transportation and utilities

When most of the leaders, managers, and employees are men, the work environment presents specific challenges for women, such as ingrained stereotypes and assumptions. With these additional complications, why would women choose to work in a male-dominated environment? Some women are passionate about a specific profession because it's a family legacy or it aligns well with their talents and experience. Some are recruited or inspired by a mentor or professor. Others are inherently born with a God-given passion and ability for a particular industry without regard for what the world thinks about women in that field.

Personally, I stumbled into a male-led industry and organization. I started out in a small company in the outdoor industry, which at the time was an industry represented largely by men. That small company grew up around me and evolved into a sizable international business. The company and the industry were both run and managed by men for most of my career. I was one of the only female leaders, and it took me years to realize how the workplace demographic affected many aspects of the job—not just for me, but for all the women who worked there.

What's important to remember is that you have the right to choose where you want to work. You don't have to avoid companies or industries where men are in the majority. But you'll want to be aware of potential challenges and unique opportunities so you can successfully navigate the landscape. Not all scenarios are found in every company or industry, but knowing what you may encounter can help you make informed responses and decisions.

CHALLENGING SCENARIOS YOU MAY ENCOUNTER

High exposure to gender bias and harmful stereotypes. It's important to remember that biases are simply an opinion that someone forms about another person, usually based on a lack of information or a misunderstood stereotype about them. One gender bias about women is that they overreact and are too emotional.

"Hannah" is a customer service manager in the oil and gas industry. She told me about a time she led a video meeting involving her peers. She asked everyone to wrap up their conversations so the meeting could start. One man remarked, "Wow. Someone's feeling bossy today." Hannah advised her colleague that his remark was inappropriate and then promptly started the meeting. Later, she had a private conversation with this person and told him that what he said wasn't okay. She felt confident he wouldn't have said this to a male leader and asked him not to make those types of remarks to her in the future.

I told her she did the right thing by not letting her colleague's behavior slide. She was professional but made it clear that the remark wasn't acceptable. Hannah said she felt empowered by that particular confrontation. We agreed, though, that over time, dealing with gender-biased remarks can lead to job dissatisfaction and stress.

Women may also face gender stereotypes like being disproportionately relegated to jobs and tasks that yield no return on investment. Simply put, women are more likely than men to be given dead-end work like planning social events, organizing schedules, and taking notes.[7] These tasks don't give women the opportunity to show their strengths and don't set them up for promotions or success.

Difficulty getting promoted and receiving raises. Women have made a lot of progress to achieve equal pay and opportunities, but when this struggle happens inside a male-dominated industry, the odds are stacked against them. According to a survey by the Pew Research Center, 35 percent of women in male-led industries earned less than men compared to 22 percent in industries where there were more women than men.[8] The same survey showed that only 48 percent of women in these industries are treated fairly relative to recruitment and hiring and only 38 percent say women are treated fairly relative to promotions.[9]

No matter how thorough, studies still represent an incomplete sampling. I know women leaders in male-dominated industries who have been paid very fairly and others who haven't. My personal experience matches what the research says.

In one situation, I was a director overseeing more than half of the company and one of two female leaders. During a lunch conversation with a new (male) director, I learned his starting salary was much higher than mine, and I'd been with the company for seven years. He had one direct report and shared his relief that the starting salary at our small company was much more competitive than he'd hoped. I hid my shock but resolved to negotiate a higher salary when the time was strategically right.

This wasn't an isolated situation, but because I chose to remain in the industry, I also chose to sharpen my negotiation skills and tactics. If this is where you are, I invite you to read chapter 9 on negotiating. I think it will help!

Adopting a scarcity mindset. Women who work in male-led industries are extremely stressed and spend a lot of time in a defensive mode or fighting for a place. They may develop a scarcity mindset, as though there could be only "one seat at the table."[10] They see the pie as too small already, and as a result, they can be guarded around other women or can even treat them unfairly.

Another outcome is that in these industries where women-led mentoring programs are desperately needed, they're often absent.[11]

Between men who are apathetic about elevating women and women who are too afraid to make space for one another, support can be lacking. Women end up feeling isolated, which feeds into the scarcity mindset.

Leading Through the Challenges

These challenges may seem overwhelming, but they're not impossible. Women have differing tolerance levels, motivations, and backgrounds. Factors like personality and origin story play into whether a woman thinks the challenge of working in a male-led industry is worth it. We have a right to work in the industries and companies we choose, and it's always better to be informed than not. One thing is certain: leaders who are in the minority as women have to create the changes we want to see.

Keep in mind that just because your company doesn't have policies focused on equity and inclusion doesn't mean leadership isn't open to them. You may have a boss or leadership team who is open to change, but if they aren't facing the same problems, the issues won't be a priority. They still may support your ideas if you lay the foundation. While workplace cultures can feel concrete or forever fixed in place, there are ways to chip away and create something new. Here are a few suggestions that will help:

It's hard for change to happen when the only people advocating for it are the ones affected by it.

Lead by example. Make sure everyone on your team participates equally in tasks that are typically assigned to women. For example, create a rotating schedule so note takers, meeting organizers, or social planners take turns. Encourage men you lead to be advocates and help them understand what this means. Be prepared to answer questions like, "What can men do to help women eliminate gender bias in the workplace?" Host a lunch-and-learn to highlight issues women struggle with, such as negotiating a raise or self-promotion, and provide helpful tips from your own experience. Invite men and women to attend!

You don't have to relinquish your feminine attributes or forfeit your emotions at work. God intended for you to use the skills and talents that you have, and He didn't mistakenly make you a female.

Enlist the help of men. It's hard for change to happen when the only people advocating for it are the ones affected by it. To get the needle to move, you'll need to ask men to support your efforts. In my case, a male friend and peer volunteered to take notes whenever he was in a meeting with me and my boss. Otherwise, my boss insisted I take notes at every meeting, even when I was leading it. My friend's actions helped change the culture.

Have conversations with coworkers about issues like gender equity and inclusion. You can't change what you don't talk about, and a conversation is a simple, easy way to start making progress. Urge men to be sponsors for women. As senior leaders with influence and credentials, sponsors can help women progress in their careers by vouching for them and recommending them for important projects and initiatives.

Become a pioneer and advocate for other women. To support women in a male-dominated work culture, you have to first understand what the specific gender gaps are. Every company has its own opportunities and constraints. Be mindful, so you'll know where to start and how to prioritize. If there isn't a formal mentorship program, create one or advocate for other women informally.

Pay attention to your company's culture. By nature, women are interrupted more than men, even when they're leading a meeting. When you notice female colleagues being interrupted, interject. Insist that they be allowed to finish. Coach women on how to regain control of conversations when interrupted. If, for example, a woman is leading a meeting and keeps getting interrupted by the same person, she can say something like, "I appreciate your enthusiasm and want to hear more later. For now, let's stay on topic." Ironically, women will probably have to interrupt to stop interruptions. Explain that this may feel counterintuitive at first, but they'll get used to it. My experience is that after you consistently and kindly (but firmly) stop interrupters, they become more aware and interruptions decrease.

Speak up when comments are made that contribute to gender bias. Ask questions to understand the bias and break down barriers. I was once waiting for a meeting to start, when a male employee made a remark about a female manager who was working from home temporarily. She and her husband were sorting out new routines around their newborn baby. The remark was about how we needed to start looking for someone to replace the manager since her commitment was "on the way down." The manager wasn't part of the meeting, so I said, "I'm curious. Has something happened to indicate her performance is slipping?" He didn't have a chance to answer because the meeting started, but I invited him to lunch so we could talk more. I listened to his viewpoint, which he admitted was an assumption. When I explained that women who are mothers are not automatically less committed or competent, he was willing to hear me out, especially when I reminded him that I was a mom too.

> **Being part of a group focused on empowering and helping other women will inspire you to do the same!**

Join professional organizations for women. Seek out organizations that offer support, community, and practical resources. Because I was in the outdoor industry, I joined the Outdoor Industries Women's Coalition, which proved to be a powerful resource in many ways, including salary studies, networking, and best practices. There are also organizations for women specific to their fields, such as supply chain, engineering, and accounting. Even if other women don't work in the exact same industry or field, being part of a group focused on empowering and helping other women will inspire you to do the same!

Drive changes in culture by changing policies. Work to ensure your organization has family-friendly work policies like flexible schedules, maternity/paternity leave, and breastfeeding accommodations for nursing moms. Be aware that even though federal law protects some rights, such as those held by breastfeeding mothers at work, that doesn't mean the company is in compliance. If there hasn't been a focus on family-friendly policies, these laws get pushed to the back of the line, and it may be up to you as a leader to get them prioritized.

Lobby for fair hiring practices. Make sure that candidate screening practices aren't biased and that interview processes are standardized. My husband worked for a large company where the human resources department was given detailed qualifications all candidates had to meet. But the department was also tasked with searching for diverse candidates. If certain job fairs or schools only yielded male candidates, the department broadened their search. The goal was to provide hiring managers with equally qualified, diverse candidates. Company policy also required diversity on the interview team.

If you're feeling like your own company policies and practices have a long way to go, I understand. Know that these important, impactive changes will take time, but your involvement and leadership will make a difference. As 4word founder Diane Paddison says in *Work, Pray, Love,* "With so many of us out there adding value to . . . businesses and other enterprises, employers have begun listening to us. Companies know that to attract the best workers from fully one-half of the talent pool, they need to find ways to accommodate women who have families."[12] Take heart and start to build.

SACRED WORK

Whenever the LORD raised up a judge over Israel, he was with that judge and rescued the people from their enemies throughout the judge's lifetime. For the LORD took pity on his people, who were burdened by oppression and suffering.

JUDGES 2:18 NLT

If we thought we were alone as Christian women leading in cultures typically governed by men, we need to look no further than Deborah. In the book of Judges, the word *judge* refers to a military and political leader of Israel who was empowered and chosen by God.[13] Judges led Israel through a dark and troubled historical time.[14] Deborah is the only female judge mentioned in the Bible, and her ability to resolve twenty years of conflict resulted in forty years of peace (see Judges 4 and 5).

Known for her wise counsel, conflict resolution skills, and leadership, Deborah was also a prophetess. The general of the Israelite army, Barak, respected her and followed her orders. Deborah both commanded and compelled Barak and had no problem riding into battle beside him and 10,000 soldiers (see Judges 4 and 5). She was a courageous warrior, spokesperson, and woman of God. Her character, qualifications, and talents are exactly what the Israelites needed at that precise time.

Deborah's story reminds us that God has always used His people where they're at, and there is no situation too sticky for Him. When the odds are stacked against us, God is just getting started! Even though Scripture indicates all other judges had been men, God had no issue raising up a woman as a judicial, political, and military leader. The forty years of peace Israel experienced under Deborah's reign were extremely rare; yet they happened. God worked through her to lead and rescue His people.

Fast forward 3,300 years to the present: You're not riding into a physical battle, but you may be battle-weary working in an industry or organization where women are underrepresented. If you start to question your role, the place and timing of your current work assignment, or your ability to effect change—remember Deborah. You have these things in common with her: a direct line to God, the power of God with you, and a commission that came straight from Him.

Deborah's song of praise to God closes with this benediction: "But may all who love you [LORD] be like the sun when it rises in its strength" (Judg. 5:31).

∫

8

Promoting Yourself with Confidence

I praise you because I am fearfully and wonderfully made;
your works are wonderful, I know that full well.

PSALM 139:14

I n 2014, I started a foundation called Sacred Work, where I offer free career and leadership coaching for women in the workplace. I've found that one of the top areas women struggle with is promoting their achievements to pave the way for career advancement and pay increases. Whether for a job interview, an annual performance review, or to prepare for a future role, women are uncomfortable providing positive self-assessments. I understand this discomfort because I spent years overcoming it.

We are our Creator's workmanship and Scripture says we were made in His image (see Eph. 2:10 and Gen. 1:27). While God hand-crafted us with unique talents and skills, women generally hold back from giving themselves credit for what they offer the world. Self-promotion in the workplace comes down to describing what we've accomplished to help the company and serve others. Without it, professionals are far less likely to receive raises, advancements, or access to pivotal projects. So why do women struggle with it?

WHY DO WOMEN STRUGGLE WITH SELF-PROMOTION?

Mary Guirovich is the CEO and founder of the company My Promotion Plan (MPP). Her company empowers women to recognize their leadership potential and move forward in their careers. MPP was birthed from a season in Mary's professional journey when she found herself striving for a promotion that seemed out of reach. She had a string of accomplishments on record and was a top producer, but she couldn't gain traction to move ahead. Through prayer, God prompted her to create a promotion plan. He provided instruction about how to organize it and what to include. The day after she submitted it, Mary was appointed vice president of operations and then COO.

As the CEO of her own company today, she shares this same plan with other women so they can realize their dreams. I interviewed Mary and asked her why women, especially Christians, have a hard time promoting themselves. Here are highlights from our conversation:[1]

We hold misconceptions about humility. Women often feel guilty if we call attention to our triumphs because we see this as prideful. If we make our accomplishments known, we think we're being egotistical. We may have been taught that humility means not pointing out our successes, because that sounds like bragging; however, this is not the definition of humility God shows us. He asks us to be humble by acknowledging we need Him (see Prov. 22:4). Humility is a heart posture. We don't rank ourselves above someone else or position ourselves as better than them. We don't think less of ourselves or other people, because our hearts recognize who we are in relation to God and others (see Rom. 12:3 and 1 Peter 5:5). Dimming our performance doesn't fit into that space, and neither does hiding the talents and gifts God gave us.

Pastor and author Todd Wilson writes, "Contrary to popular opinion, humility doesn't force you to make a dozen downward adjustments in the way you view yourself. You don't need to downplay the fact you aced the SAT or took home a fistful of firsts at the state swim meet. You don't need to hide the fact you graduated *summa cum laude* from Harvard, or that you can play the cello like Yo-Yo Ma, write poetry like Goethe, have an uncanny ability to remember names, [or] run a Fortune 500 company. . . . Being humble doesn't require you to deny reality."[2]

We get stuck in loops. Mary explains loops as "rewarded behaviors we repeat over and over."[3] When a situation has a positive outcome, we repeat the behavior that got us there. Unfortunately, these loops hinder women from promoting themselves when the actions we took in the past are no longer relevant. For example, we worked extra hard and got noticed, so we work harder. As we progress in our careers, working harder isn't enough. We won't land a career upgrade just because we worked more hours than anyone else.

Another loop centers on the idea of waiting. Traditional society trains us to wait: We wait our turn. We wait to be chosen (for so many things). We wait to be told we're good enough for a raise or the next step in the career ladder. If waiting has paid off once or twice, we hold our position. When waiting doesn't yield results, we tell ourselves we must not be ready, or talented enough, or a good fit.

> When waiting doesn't yield results, we tell ourselves we must not be ready, or talented enough, or a good fit. These loops paralyze us.

These loops paralyze us. Do any of these scenarios feel familiar to you, as they do to me? Early in my career, there were many times I wish I would have stopped the roller coaster instead of letting it exhaust and dizzy me. Awareness breaks the cycle.

We believe we're giving ourselves credit, but we're not. Because women tend to be more comfortable giving credit to other people, we put the spotlight on them and mention ourselves as an afterthought (or not at all). Let's say you manage a large project, and it's a success. Deadlines were hit. Budgets were met. Employees are happy. When you talk about it with your boss, you focus on what the team did well. You give credit to everyone else and aren't even aware you're detracting credit from yourself. One reason we do this connects back to misunderstood humility.

The other reason is we assume our boss already knows our contribution to the project, departmental feat, or whatever undertaking we championed. We think our part was obvious, so we don't elaborate. In reality, our bosses are busy and distracted. They don't have time to interpret what we don't say. If we want them to see our part, we need to point it out. Leaders perform a disservice to everyone when they make themselves invisible because invisible people are hard-pressed to make a difference or an impact.

WHAT DOES RESEARCH SAY?

Studies consistently show men are comfortable speaking favorably about their performance at work, while women tend to shy away from doing so. Women give credit to their teams or think their achievements should stand for themselves.[4]

Christine Exley at Harvard Business School and Judd Kessler at the Wharton School conducted a study with this conclusion: "In every setting we explored, we observed a substantial gender gap in self-promotion: Women systematically provided less favorable assessments of their own past performance and potential future ability than equally performing men."[5]

Even when women outperformed other employees in tangible,

measurable ways, they still shied away from touting their successes. For the past decade, study after study shows a persistent gender gap in self-promotion.[6] There's a reason behavioral scientists continue to study this issue: it's a persistent, consistent problem. No matter how isolated you feel in your struggle with self-promoting, you're clearly not alone. It's not just you!

The importance of knowing your "why." It's comforting to realize there are reasons behind your struggle. Once you recognize and acknowledge the "why," you're a step closer to removing whatever obstacle stands between you and your best professional outcome. If you don't understand *why* you behave in certain ways, you'll find it more difficult to change. Breaking down the "why" gives you a starting point for change.

Origin stories and societal norms play a part. Societal and cultural norms carve out a behavioral path, which is then reinforced and perpetuated in the professional realm. I was brought up in a home where being a "good girl" meant working hard, being quiet, and not drawing attention to myself. This helped me thrive as a student and athlete, but it didn't serve me well in a work setting. Many women were brought up in similar ways.

Family and school dynamics taught them that being outspoken about their abilities would lead to negative reactions.[7] When they talked about themselves in positive ways, they may have been called "arrogant" or made to feel not part of the team and even unlikeable. Other girls could have led the way in criticizing them, which took the discomfort to new levels.

This behavior transfers readily into the work environment. As we grow into adults, the social conditioning we experienced as children may get reinforced by colleagues or people who view us as competition. Naturally, we don't like how that feels, so we quietly perform, and hope others will do the right thing—and notice.

REFRAMING SELF-PROMOTION

Now that you better understand why women struggle with self-promotion, here are four tips to help you reframe it, so you're more comfortable doing it:

1. **Use different words.** If "self-promote" and "self-promotion" keep tripping you up, try embracing the concept without embracing the verbiage; change the wording. Think about terms like "highlight my wins," "emphasize my contributions," "use my voice," and "identify my skills."

2. **View yourself as helpful, not prideful.** The interview panel, your boss, your potential boss, the board of directors—they're all short on time and attention. Like you, they're juggling a lot at home and work. The hallmark achievement you listed on your résumé or performance review could easily get overlooked. Don't assume they'll see it and don't make them dig for it. Pointing out our contributions helps us, but it also helps leaders who need to know (quickly) what we're bringing to the table.

3. **Focus on facts, not feelings.** Women I've mentored say they hesitate to self-promote because it feels too emotional and risky. Many were conditioned to keep their feelings away from work, almost to an extreme. God created us with emotions, and we don't have to repress our feelings at work; we just have to use them constructively. Be enthusiastic but focus on facts to talk about what you've accomplished. Rely on numbers, such as years of experience, sales goals exceeded, dollars saved, efficiency gained, or retention rates achieved.

4. **Know that expanding your reach expands God's reach.** Your work has a purpose and God gave you talents to fulfill

it. The more you use your talents to serve other people and the organization you work for, the more you increase your influence. God didn't create you to live small. Small spaces feel safe, but you can't live out the full impact God created you to make when you sit in spaces the size of your comfort zone. When you shine the light on your capabilities, you're creating opportunities to bring more value to the company and people you serve. As we walk humbly and rightly before God and others, we will boldly become the women God created us to be, and our lives will keep pointing people to Him, our Creator.

PRACTICAL WAYS TO PROMOTE YOURSELF

Suppose you've warmed up to the idea of being more vocal about your efforts. Or maybe you've decided you won't wait for someone to present you with an advancement opportunity; you're ready to go after it. These concepts aren't as uncomfortable as they were at first. But you're battling old habits, and there's a fear-based voice in the back of your mind saying, "You shouldn't _____ [take credit, talk about your strengths, speak up]."

Maybe you're willing to forge ahead, but the first step is hazy. Or you don't like where you are in your career, but it feels safer to work harder than to change. Your mind may have churning questions like these:

- Why does it feel like I can never make this happen?
- What if my boss or coworkers don't like this?
- How can I share my strengths without feeling like I'm just bragging?
- How do I start?

Asking questions is part of the process, and now that you've asked them, let them go! You're ready to move on, and I put together practical steps to help you get started. I included ideas from Mary's book, *God's Not Done with You: How to Advance Your Career and Live in Abundance*. Do you remember Mary? As the CEO and founder of the company, My Promotion Plan, she's another fantastic resource to help you get the promotion you want and deserve.

I Want a Promotion!

1. **Decide what you want and build a plan.** Take time to decide what it is you really want. Is it more money, more flexibility, or more opportunities? Give yourself permission to put words to your dream and map out what it takes to get there. Once you set a goal and write it down, you have a starting point. Then create an actionable plan based on your goal. Mary calls this the "Career Advancement Journey" (CAJ), and it includes documenting the future role you want, the responsibilities of the role, and the training or experience you need to get there.[8] Mary says this simple exercise is powerful because "it brings the possibility of a promotion closer to you; it becomes attainable."[9]

2. **Communicate what you want to your boss.** The "hard work equals reward" loop only leads to frustration, burnout, and resentment. Don't work long hours, waiting for your boss to bring up career advancement. Be direct and communicate your professional goals with them. Once they understand your intentions, your boss is more likely to think of you when opportunities come up or the role you want becomes available. You want your boss thinking about how you would fill a role, even before one opens up.

3. **Say yes to what you want.** Once you have a goal and a plan, and you've communicated them to your boss, align your actions with your goal. Mary explains how women often want to please others and be team players.[10] So they say yes to social tasks, admin duties, and helping in ways that don't support the work they ultimately want to do. Volunteering is a good attribute, but if you spend too much time volunteering, you get closer to burnout and further from your goal. Your most important work needs to fill the majority of your time.

I'm Ready to Share My Accomplishments. How Do I Start?

1. **Create a portfolio.** Look for an upcoming event where you can show off your accomplishments or ways you've made a positive impact. Are you about to celebrate the end of a large project? Is it time for your performance review? Are you up for a promotion or interviewing for a new job? As you prepare for a specific event, use the momentum to start documenting your successes in a portfolio. Then you can edit and use the portfolio in a variety of situations.

2. **Involve your circle of influence.** Make a list of leaders and decision-makers in your professional circle with whom you can share your work victories. These may be people in your company, network, or industry. Think about your current position and where you'd like to be in the future. You may want to advance with your company or move to a different industry. Maybe you're happy in your current role, but you want to push for more compensation or involvement in high-profile projects. Who can help these changes happen? Who is empowered to make decisions that move you toward these goals?

3. **Brainstorm ways to share contributions with your circle of influence.** Once you have your portfolio and list of people, think about the exposure you want and match items from your portfolio to people on your list. In many cases, you can share your contributions in a way that serves others. Here are a few examples:

- Hold a lunch-and-learn for people at your company where you share best practices from a recent project. Everyone attending can benefit from this.
- Share a professional win on LinkedIn with important lessons learned.
- Identify one or two past accomplishments that show your ability to bring value to a future project or position. Have a preliminary conversation with the project owner or hiring manager to talk about what you could contribute.
- Identify how to benefit your company using one of your proven strengths and share this idea with your boss.
- Find an industry publication and submit a case study describing a project you led.

HOW TO HELP OTHER WOMEN CELEBRATE THEIR SUCCESSES

Women leaders are perfectly positioned to use their breakthroughs about self-promotion to elevate and promote other women. Because social conditioning and some stereotypes are formulated by other women, women can also help deconstruct both. When you promote women and help them celebrate their achievements, you begin to change the culture within your organization. You defeat old stereotypes and ways of thinking, which helps women become more comfortable shining and less comfortable shying away. There are so many ways we can inspire other women to live boldly in the workplace. Here are a few ideas:

- Send out a company-wide email recognizing specific achievements.
- Invite women to take part in special projects and point out the distinct skill set or talent that qualifies them to be involved.
- Recognize individuals in all-hands meetings, citing their company or departmental contributions.
- Recognize women across the company; don't limit recognition to your own department.
- Address negative remarks made about women who share their accomplishments. Don't let these remarks stand.
- Post a shout-out on LinkedIn, spotlighting a peer for her accomplishments.

SACRED WORK

Not to us, LORD, not to us but to your name be the glory,
because of your love and faithfulness.

PSALM 115:1

Climbing the corporate ladder may seem like a worldly endeavor. It can feel dishonoring to Christ when you promote yourself or pursue a promotion, but neither runs contrary to your faith. God examines the motive behind your actions. If you're concerned that showcasing your talents or efforts might not align with what God has in mind, ask the Holy Spirit to search your motivations and reveal what needs to be surrendered. As He instructs you, keep a posture of humility and gratitude.

Psalm 115 consistently points to God as the provider, blesser, and protector. It cautions the Israelites against worshiping powerless, lifeless gods. We too should guard our hearts against bowing to empty idols, like vanity (pursuing promotions for the wrong reasons) and self-sufficiency (thinking we know best and don't need God's help). The Holy Spirit will faithfully show us places where worldly motivations take up too much heart space. He will also affirm when the steps we want to take for advancement are steps in the right direction.

The psalmist continues, "The highest heaven belongs to the LORD, but he gave the earth to all people" (Ps. 115:16 CEB[11]). God created the earth and then trusted us enough to make us stewards over it. We're stewards of where we work and the teams we lead.

Think about how much God trusts you and believes in your abilities. Every good and perfect gift, talent, and accomplishment comes from Him and points to Him. But the enemy doesn't want God glorified, so he trips you up with guilt, insecurity, and confusion to keep you small. Once you realize God expands your reach to expand His reach, you're free to pursue the ambitions He's called you to while remaining confident in your faith.

My prayer for you: Father, help the woman reading these words embrace the talent, skills, and gifts You've blessed her with. Help her realize You are proud of her! She is Your creation. Grant her confidence as she steps forward into the next role, project, or assignment You have planned for her. Give her clarity and help her release all false notions of guilt and humility. Thank You for what You're going to do next in her life and career!

9

Negotiating to Win

Often we fear negotiating. We think we'll upset our boss or miss out
on a job opportunity. The truth is that those who negotiate are often
seen as more competent or even more sought after.[1]

MARY E. GUIROVICH, AUTHOR AND CEO OF MY PROMOTION PLAN

A bright young woman sat across from me at dinner, extremely
upset because her annual raise was less than expected. Again.
I asked, "What exactly did you expect?"

"That my boss would give me what I deserve."

"What do you deserve?"

She stared at me . . . down at her plate . . . back at me.

For a moment, I looked at her face and saw my own when I was
her age and found out I was getting a paltry 2 percent raise. The
company was going gangbusters, but I couldn't form an argument
for a higher percentage and didn't know what to do next.

I shared this memory with my mentee, reassuring her I understood how she felt. Then I gently told her that until she knew what
she deserved and asked for it, her boss wouldn't give it to her. In
order to get the pay she wanted, she needed to identify a figure, do
the prep work, and then ask for it. She explained that for the past two
years, her boss was late with her pay increases. He didn't apologize

but simply emailed the digital form to her, saying, "I'll make it retro-active." This made her feel powerless.

You can't negotiate if you never make it to the table.

I asked, "What would happen if you didn't sign the form and scheduled a meeting with him to discuss your pay?"

"I'm not sure that's an option."

"Of course it is. Your boss may be busy, or this may be a power play, but either way, you have the ability to stop it."

This young woman isn't alone. Many women shy away from pay-related discussions.[2] Women leaders barter with customers, suppliers, consultants, bosses, and peers, but in general, they struggle to negotiate on behalf of themselves.[3]

WHY ARE WOMEN UNCOMFORTABLE NEGOTIATING FOR THEMSELVES?

The women I mentor tell me they carry out a rigorous approach when discussing terms on behalf of their company or for an individual employee. Yet when it's time to advocate for themselves, anxiety can overwhelm and make the first step difficult. They view self-advocating as optional while advocating for others is not. Some say they walk into a compensation meeting believing their boss will do what's fair. When the amount isn't what they think is equitable, they feel too uncomfortable to push back. Research shows these responses and the reasons behind them are all too common.

Why understand the "why"? One way to counteract negative feelings about negotiation is to understand them. Where did they come from? Why do we have them? Once we understand our feelings, we can manage them, so they're working for us and not against us. Once we understand our responses, we're better positioned to change them. Let's jump in!

Women avoid the process because they feel unprepared or aren't sure how to prepare. I remember a time when I didn't know salary negotiations were an option. Even after I realized I *could* negotiate pay and benefits, I had no idea where to start or what a successful negotiation looked like. On top of these questions sat a lingering fear of questioning authority figures (like bosses and corporations), especially when it came to compensation.

Avoidance can also happen if our first attempt to negotiate left us feeling embarrassed and unprepared. Have you ever put in the work to ask for a raise, but the results weren't what you'd hoped for?

One director told me that she labored through the preparations to transact her first raise, but she wasn't confident or clear on the process. She attempted to fit in her "ask" at the end of a standing meeting with her boss because she wanted to be respectful of his busy schedule. He interrupted saying they'd have to talk later, and she came away feeling inadequate and humiliated. She found it difficult to shake these feelings, so she didn't want to try again. Other women find themselves blindsided, as in the case of my earlier mentee, whose boss delivered raises late and without discussion.

> While you may be able to detach yourself when lobbying for others, it's hard to step back when you're lobbying for yourself.

Brokering a deal is stressful because women are emotionally invested in the outcome. Fear plays a powerful role in negotiations because you aren't sure of the outcome. How will your boss react? What if you win? What if you lose? Will your boss be upset? Will they tell other people or treat you differently?

While you may be able to detach yourself when lobbying for others, it's hard to step back when you're lobbying for yourself. You're advocating for a personal gain that will benefit you or your family, and you feel the weight of what you might lose. These unknowns feed into your fear and emotional distress, which is uncomfortable. As a result, you may avoid the situation altogether.

When women ask for a pay raise, it may come at a social cost.[4] Research supports that women who advocate for pay increases are often faced with backlash and can be seen as unlikeable and aggressive.[5] When women wrangle pay or benefits for others, this backlash diminishes. In fact, people view assertiveness favorably when women advocate for others.[6] These contrasting responses condition women to avoid situations that could lead to conflict, damaged work relationships, or poor outcomes. They avoid self-advocating because the social cost leaves them feeling professionally and relationally bankrupt.

Sometimes women attempt to secure a higher salary, are turned down, and then treated differently afterward. The first time I tried negotiating a raise, I was a teenager, working at McDonald's. The manager not only laughed at me, but she also told other workers and managers I thought I was better than everyone else. The hubbub eventually died down and I recovered, but that experience followed me around much longer than it should have.

The bottom line: Did you recognize yourself in any of the "why" scenarios? Be encouraged, because you're not alone. Other women, including me, have stood where you are, and I'm here to tell you: you are capable of overcoming whatever has you feeling unequipped or stuck. Keep reading, because a successful negotiation is well within your grasp!

HOW TO NEGOTIATE SKILLFULLY AND WITH CONFIDENCE

Like other skills you've mastered as a leader, negotiation is learned, and you *can* overcome the fear and discomfort you associate with it. As your knowledge and experience increase, your fear and discomfort will decrease. Here are five strategies to help you build your confidence and get the results you want:

1. Understand what matters most to you.

Erica Dvorak, founder of Faith & Gather, spent much of her career as a marketing expert working for startups and Fortune 500 companies. She shared a perspective I'd never considered. She said, "A lot of times women think they want the title, salary, or raise, but they don't think about what they want for their life."[7] More money is one benefit, but it's not the only benefit. A woman may button up a significant raise only to find the accompanying workload cripples the other parts of her life.

Erica suggests envisioning what you want your personal *and* professional life to be like. You may want more flexibility so you have dedicated time with your family. Working remotely might be appealing if commuting is problematic. You may want to impact change at your company, so you want a position where this is possible. Erica says, "Be in tune with what you value the most right now and let priorities guide what you're asking for."[8]

2. Identify past wins.

Whether or not you realize it, you've probably been brokering deals throughout your career. You can take the same principles you used to succeed in other scenarios and apply them for yourself. As a junior leader, I spent hours researching, strategizing, and even role-playing to prepare for the bargaining I did for someone else. But when advocating for my own pay, I sold myself short.

I invite you to take a few minutes and brainstorm any negotiations you've handled in your career, such as better payment terms, strong signing packages, or better rates from health insurance companies. You may have spearheaded non-monetary agreements too, like persuading your boss to let you restructure a department or lobbying other leaders toward the best business software.

List your wins and then jot down the tactics you used. This exercise creates a track record that can outpace emotions and change how you see yourself as a negotiator. A change in mindset sets the stage for a positive experience.

3. Stop viewing negotiation as manipulative or adversarial.

Women sometimes shy away from bargaining because they see it as manipulative, but you can be strategic without being manipulative. Strategy means you understand yourself, the other party, and the game plan. When you strategize, you develop a logical approach and have a clear idea of the possible outcomes for all parties involved.

An adversarial climate only brews from a scarcity mindset. This mindset views the only outcome as one party winning and one party losing, but hammering out a fair, workable agreement for both parties is absolutely doable!

Part of a successful agreement is understanding what you have to offer, not just what you have to gain. As Erica says, "You can't just ask yourself, 'What's in it for me?' You have to also ask yourself, 'What's in it for my company?'"[9] You're bringing something to the table, and you're going to walk away with something. There's nothing manipulative or adversarial about that.

4. Evaluate the macro-environment.

Whatever is going on in the economy, industry, and labor market creates a backdrop that impacts your terms. "Ann" is the director of talent acquisition at a high-tech company, and I asked her why it was so important for women to consider the macro-environment as they approach the bargaining table. She immediately responded, "One word captures it: leverage."

Let's say there's a labor shortage, such as the Great Resignation of 2021, when employees had an advantage. With a competitive job market and robust economy in the backdrop, a woman can approach the table with added confidence. She can expect to have more leeway and options, but the flip side is also true. If the job market is flooded and the economy weak, she needs to take these factors into account. The ability to work remotely more often or have a more flexible schedule may need to move up on the list, and higher pay may need to move lower.

5. Evaluate your company's environment.

You also want to consider what's going on inside your specific organization. For example, is the company getting ready to switch to all-remote work? Or from remote to hybrid? If you manage a team, you have leverage because your company won't want to make a big change while scrambling to replace leaders or worrying about losing them. Are there big projects ahead where you'll be a major contributor? Is your company preparing for a new software system, a re-branding, or a relocation? If so, you have leverage. When companies implement major changes, they want their leadership team intact.

Weigh your evaluation of the macro-environment against what's going on in your company environment to assess your net leverage. Knowledge is power: when you can zoom in and out on your company's environment, you can use the information to determine your next step.

Summary: Keep these five strategies in mind as you approach the negotiation process. Know your priorities, give yourself credit for past negotiations, and remember that it's okay to bring your "savvy" to the table! Next, we'll go through an eight-step negotiation process that's worked for me and the women I mentor.

EIGHT STEPS TO GUIDE YOU THROUGH THE NEGOTIATION PROCESS

Payscale's *2023 Gender Pay Gap Report* showed "women earn 82 cents for every $1 men earn when comparing all women to all men."[10] While there's a lot of speculation about the reasons behind this gap, the issue remains *in part* because, as we've discussed, women are reluctant to assert themselves for better pay.[11]

I've created a step-by-step, manageable method that's based on facts and data. The best way to eliminate emotions that aren't serving you is to crowd them out with facts, which is exactly what you'll do as you walk through each step. This method requires extensive research, so set up a spreadsheet or outline to organize your data and findings. When you're finished, you'll be able to cull data from the most pertinent findings to include in the presentation you deliver to your boss. Here are the steps:

1. **Identify the salary range for your position in a similarly sized company**. If your company isn't 100 percent remote, consider your geographical location as part of your research. Find your state's annual compensation report, and the wage and salary reports provided by your state's department of workforce services. From these resources, you'll gain a comprehensive understanding of merit and across-the-board pay increases, which will better prepare you for the salary discussion. Make sure you document your sources in case your boss asks for them.

Even if you work remotely and your company is head-quartered in another state, it's important to know *your* state's average compensation because those numbers are what your employer has to compete with to keep you. Document salary ranges from a variety of sources to create a litmus test.

2. **Understand how your experience affects your salary.** Some websites have an online calculator to help you esti-mate how your relevant experience affects your salary. Even if sites don't ask for your experience, you can still make a close estimate. Let's say you do your research and establish a range of $70–80 thousand. If you have ten years of expe-rience, assume you're at the upper end of the range. Your boss may ask you why you feel the company should pay you at the higher end, and experience is part of the equation.

3. **Understand the relevancy of your degree.** Most sites will ask you to select your degree as part of the overall calcu-lation. Having a bachelor's degree unrelated to your field of work doesn't normally impact a salary calculation. If your graduate degree seems outside the scope of your job, be prepared to explain how it brings value. A degree that doesn't seem relevant to your boss could become a sticking point in the negotiation.

4. **Know your company's total benefits package.** Refer to the US Bureau of Labor Statistics, the workforce services for your state, or an industry-specific report for data to see how your benefits compare to those at companies in your industry. How much you pay for health insurance, the type of retirement and cafeteria plans offered, and the option for a flexible schedule are all examples of benefits you want to consider. They're part of your overall compensation, so know what they are and how they rank against other companies.

5. **Identify what you've done to add value to the company.**
Whether you're brokering a starting salary or trying to land
a raise or promotion, you need to identify the tangible contributions you've made in your career or profession. How
have you increased your company's sales, profits, efficiency,
or employee engagement? What additional responsibilities
did you take on and what were the results?

My husband, George, has worked for several large companies, including Toyota and Philips. If you're negotiating
a raise, he advises that you first quantify your company's
expectations and then quantify your performance against
those expectations. Saying, "I reduced operating costs" is
too general. By what percentage? How much money did you
save? Does this number match up to what your boss wanted
you to do? The most impactful results are measurable results.

6. **Prioritize your "asks" and how they affect the company.**
Make a prioritized list of three things you want to ask for.
Don't limit your list to salary figures or percentage increases.
Think about what's most important to you. Would a title
change help you build your résumé so you can find a more
desirable position later on? Maybe you want to build your
future by building expertise, so you ask your employer to
cover educational expenses. Perhaps you're in a season of life
where you want more paid time off (PTO). Identify what's
most important and prioritize your list. At a minimum, your
goal is to walk away with your lowest priority ask.

7. **Create your presentation and schedule the meeting.**
Though you'll need to be able to access your documentation
and details during the meeting, your actual presentation
should be brief. Having a separate meeting emphasizes the
importance of the topic and will keep you and your boss

focused. Based on your boss's personality and communication style, you'll have to decide whether to send the presentation in advance or not. Be sure to rehearse the presentation several times and ask someone to role-play your boss and challenge your asks. You want to keep the meeting on-target and moving smoothly.

8. **Present what you're asking for with confidence!** You've done all the legwork, so now it's time to shine! Walk your boss through your presentation, and don't leave until you have an answer. If your boss says, "I'll think about this and get back to you," respond by thanking them and then ask for a firm date and put it on the calendar.

Concluding thoughts: My experience is that most bosses want to pay their employees fairly, but sometimes they don't put in the effort to advocate for employees proactively. They get busy and forget how important compensation and other benefits are to the people they lead. Even when they're more numbers-driven than people-aware, the hard facts and data will get their attention.

SACRED WORK

When an employee initiates negotiations, it's often a wake-up call for leadership. We see this in the Bible, when God uses Abigail to show us how we can use the negotiation process to benefit our bosses (see 1 Sam. 25). After her husband, Nabal, disrespects David, Abigail uses her strategic mind and her husband's misused wealth to turn the situation around. As David is on his way intent on destroying everyone in Nabal's household, Abigail fearlessly rides out to meet him. She gives David and his men a substantial peace offering, takes responsibility for what's happened, and pleads for her household to be spared. With a lot of lives hanging in the balance, Abigail brokers a deal.

After listening to her, David realizes what a terrible mistake he's about to make. He says, "Praise be to the LORD, the God of Israel, who has sent you today to meet me. May you be blessed for your good judgment and for keeping me from bloodshed this day and from avenging myself with my own hands" (vv. 32–33). Abigail's diplomatic strategies protect her household and prevent David from taking action he would later regret. She's David's wake-up call.

In a similar way, you can help your boss become more aware as a leader. Your conversation about better pay or benefits can help them realize they need to be proactive when managing and retaining talent. Pray about the outcomes you're hoping for and ask God what He wants to accomplish through you. Trust that He wants what's best for you and everyone else involved, and He will accomplish it. It's easy to forget that God sees into and cares about every corner of our lives, including the pay and benefits paid to His daughters! He cares and He is with you, dear one:

> "So do not fear, for I am with you; do not be dismayed, for I am your God. I will strengthen you and help you; I will uphold you with my righteous right hand" (Isa. 41:10).

10

When You Fail

If you have made mistakes, even serious ones, there is always another chance for you. What we call failure is not the falling down, but the staying down.[1]

MARY PICKFORD, PHILANTHROPIST AND FOUNDER OF
THE UNITED ARTISTS CORPORATION

We've all experienced the pain of failed projects, budgets, systems, and contracts. No leader or employee is immune from failure either, so what becomes important is how you respond to it. All the leaders I've mentored and talked to say personnel blunders are the most painful and hardest to recover from. But they also say these blunders teach the most powerful and lasting lessons, lessons that inform their leadership for the rest of their careers.

I couldn't agree more. My biggest leadership setback happened when I fumbled a serious personnel issue.

WHEN WE FAIL OUR EMPLOYEES

I managed a young woman who was exceptionally talented. "Amanda" was analytical, an excellent communicator, and a gifted problem solver. Employees across the company respected her and enjoyed working with her, and my decision to promote her into management was an easy one.

"Lisa," one of Amanda's direct reports, had been with the company longer. She excelled in the technical aspects of her job but told me from the start she wanted to maintain a narrow focus. She didn't have management experience and didn't want it. Her husband had a demanding job and traveled often. She needed flexible hours so she could take care of things at home, and I was happy to provide this flexibility. I touched base with Lisa before Amanda's promotion, and when we talked, she said her original career goals hadn't changed. She expressed support for my decision and thanked me for talking to her ahead of time.

Lisa had reported to me for almost a year, so Amanda and I worked on her first performance review together as part of the transition. The company's review policy required every employee to receive multi-directional feedback, which meant the people who regularly interacted with the employee completed the review. I read through Lisa's feedback from suppliers, service providers, and several departments in the company. She was praised and lauded by everyone except one person: Amanda. Amanda described Lisa's behavior as insubordinate and borderline bullying. I was perplexed, not only by the contradiction between what everyone else said and Amanda's perspective, but also because Amanda hadn't mentioned it to me.

When Amanda and I talked, she explained her silence. At first, she thought Lisa was challenging her as a new manager. Amanda ignored the sarcasm and remarks, thinking both would be short-lived. When the behavior dragged on, Amanda confronted Lisa about it and was met with defiance. I was appalled and asked, "Why didn't you come to me?"

She responded, "I didn't want to disappoint you, and I thought I could handle the situation myself. I also didn't want to feel like I was telling on her."

Amanda explained that the more she tried to work with Lisa, the more unwieldy their relationship became. Lisa started blatantly ignoring Amanda during their one-on-ones. She also stopped answering emails, and the remarks she made to Amanda became more caustic. I told Amanda I was shocked by Lisa's behavior and needed to think about the best way to handle the situation. I said, "Manage your responsibilities like you normally do, and I'll get back to you on the next steps."

I reread Lisa's feedback and was stumped. There were specific examples showing how helpful she was and how well she did her job. The problems Amanda described were at odds with all of it, and I wondered if her inexperience had led her to overreact or misinterpret interactions with Lisa.

The next day, our counterparts from the parent company abroad were on-site to work on a project, so I pushed the personnel issue to the back of the priority list. Two weeks went by. The day

> She threw her work keys at me and said, "I quit!"

our guests left, I received a call from Troy, a manager from another department. Our company didn't have a human resources department; we just contracted attorneys on an as-needed basis. As directors, we handled personnel issues within our departments. Troy said Amanda had come in that morning to file a personnel complaint against Lisa. Amanda told him about our conversation and said that because I hadn't acted, she came to him. He documented everything she told him, and that document was now in my inbox.

I felt sick during the conversation with Troy and even worse when I read the document. Clearly, Lisa's behavior had escalated, and she wasn't afraid of being held accountable for it. When Amanda first brought the issue to my attention, I had compared what she wrote to what everyone else had written: Amanda's perspective versus mine and other people's. But what about Amanda? What about the fact that she consistently showed integrity, was known for being straightforward, and had no history of making exaggerated claims about other employees? She was strong, independent, and a top performer. I rewarded all of that by neglecting to give her the support she needed *when* she needed it.

I immediately met with Amanda, apologized, and told her my plans. Then I met with Lisa, and I asked Troy to be present as a witness and to take notes. My intention was to confront her behavior, but before I could finish summarizing the problem, she stood up and said she wouldn't listen to another word. When I asked her to sit down so we could finish, she walked out and slammed the door. Troy went back to his office, and I was about to look for Lisa when she stormed in. She threw her work keys at me and said, "I quit!" Lisa left, and we never heard from her again. It was a strange, disturbing turn of events, but not too far removed from how she'd behaved with Amanda for two months. I felt I had failed them both.

DEALING WITH AND RECOVERING FROM FAILURE

It took time to rebuild my relationship with Amanda, and her confidence as a new manager had taken a big hit. The human part of me very much wanted to fast forward past what happened. I wanted to turn the page on my mess instead of dealing with it. But recovering from a leadership disaster requires intention. Intention obligates us to sit in an uncomfortable space much longer than we'd like to, because if we don't manage our mishaps, we end up making the same mistakes again.

I took the time to walk back through everything that had happened, noting what I did versus what I should have done, but didn't.

During this reflection time, I came up with a six-step plan for dealing with and recovering from leadership failures. These steps have proven helpful when I've made other work mishaps, and I offer them here in hopes they can help you work through your own missteps:

1. **Take responsibility.** Human nature is to explain away our mistakes, even if just to ourselves. In my case, I actually started telling myself, *I was super busy. I was working sixty to seventy hours a week. I couldn't have put the project on hold.* These excuses all fell flat. Instead, I needed to acknowledge my mishandling and accept responsibility for it. Justifying our failure is rooted in pride and blinds us to the reality of our mistakes and their consequences. I was honest with Amanda and told her I knew I'd handled the situation poorly. When I was uncertain, I didn't ask for help from other resources, and I delayed acting on what Amanda had disclosed. I apologized and acknowledged the consequences: Amanda had lost confidence in me and confidence in herself.

   Leslie McLeod, the vice president of a security company, talked to me about recovering from her own personnel mishap. She said, "We lay the groundwork for a stronger relationship moving forward when we acknowledge the human elements involved and how they impacted the other person."[2] When we're vulnerable in admitting our failure and expressing remorse, we contribute to an authentic culture, one where making mistakes isn't fatal. We show our humanity which helps build, or rebuild, trust.

2. **Talk to God and your mentors.** When we fail the people God called us to lead, we feel as if we've failed Him too. An important part of working through the pain is talking through it with Him. Mistakes can make us feel as if we're

no longer worthy of stewarding others, but God helps us realize He didn't call us to lead because we're worthy. His power stands in the gap when our unworthiness causes us to fall short: "He said to me, 'My grace is sufficient for you, for my power is made perfect in weakness.' Therefore I will boast all the more gladly about my weaknesses, so that Christ's power may rest on me" (2 Cor. 12:9).

We should also talk about our missteps with mentors who can help us untangle what happened, so we can maximize learning without getting bogged down or feeling defeated.

3. **Reflect on what happened.** Reflection happens when we look back a few times, learn, and move forward. Obsession happens when we look back too many times and paralyze ourselves. Reliving the mistake is not the same thing as learning from it; knowing the difference is important, so we don't slide from reflection into obsession. When we reflect, we think about what went wrong, what we learned, and what we would do differently. We also consider what God is teaching us and incorporate what our mentors had to say. Reflection propels us forward.

4. **Make changes.** While we can't change what happened in the past, we can implement changes to prevent the same fiascos from happening in the future. After taking responsibility, talking with others, and reflecting, I clearly saw the preventative changes I needed to make. I communicated these to Amanda because I wanted her to know I was taking action and not just apologizing with words.

In my situation, I was reminded that if an employee discloses a personnel issue, I needed to act immediately. Other pressing issues, like projects and visitors, must all take second priority to the people I'm entrusted to lead. If a situation is complex and I'm uncertain how to respond, I need to ask for help.

5. **Reframe the failure.** When we reframe our failure, we aren't dodging responsibility. We've already accepted responsibility and implemented changes to safeguard the future. Now it's time to change how we see the error. Mine taught me lessons I've never forgotten, lessons that shaped my leadership going forward. I stopped seeing my mistake as a shameful stain. Instead, I was grateful for the wake-up call and what I had learned from it.

   Donald R. Keough, the former president of the Coca-Cola Company, wrote a book titled *The Ten Commandments for Business Failure*. In it, he said, "We pay homage to reason, but we are held hostage to emotion."[3] If we're held hostage by shame and regret, our leadership becomes crippled. We're not strengthened by what we've learned; we're held back by what we did. By reframing our mistake, we're released from the shame and are freed to flourish again.

6. **Move forward.** After my failure with Amanda, I was tempted to check in with her frequently to ask, "How do you feel about managing your new employee?" Or "How are you and I doing?" Thankfully, a mentor had already cautioned me against doing this. In order for Amanda to move past what happened, I needed to do the same. I couldn't allow the mistake I made to become a constant marker in our relationship. Doing that would further undermine her confidence in herself and in me.

   I believed we would get past what had happened and that I could be the leader Amanda deserved. I also believed Amanda would be a successful manager. Neither Amanda nor I were content to get stuck in the shadow of my mistake.

By choice, we restarted our relationship in a way that left space for hope and new possibilities.

FAILURE AS FEEDBACK

When, oh when, will we learn to honor error?
To understand that goofs are the only way to step forward,
that really big goofs are the only way to leap forward?[4]

TOM PETERS, AUTHOR AND FOUNDER OF THE TOM PETERS COMPANY

Not all debacles involve people, however. Innovative leaders take risks, and all successful businesses are used to snafus. Teams and companies who run toward the cutting edge understand that errors are a sign of progress. People apply what they've learned and try again and again until they reach a breakthrough. Success doesn't teach us about limitations; our mistakes do. Taking risks opens the door for innovation and failure, and we need to teach our employees that it's safe to welcome both.

In my last corporate job, my final project was to design and build a new headquarters and distribution center. It was an enormous task, and I had the honor of leading a team of incredibly talented people. Besides the new buildings, we also implemented a new warehouse management system and a new traffic management system at the same time. Trailblazing times four! The stakeholders held us to the usual on-time and on-budget requirements, but they were most concerned about uninterrupted customer service and deliveries. Downtime wasn't an option. Since we were changing software, hardware, warehouse equipment, and physical locations, they were understandably nervous. They didn't want a glitch in the new system to prevent our customers from placing and receiving orders.

After talking to consultants and other companies who had taken on similar endeavors, we decided to run parallel systems: the old and the new. We'd do a soft launch of the new system, while simultaneously running the old system at the old warehouse as a backup. Our consultants told us that the exact interface we needed hadn't been attempted before, so there was some risk. My team and I pored over all the data points and chose to go for

We made just enough progress to get our hopes up. But then we hit a wall. In a short time, we had an unmanageable mess on our hands.

it. We would run two physical and systematic warehouses and then cut over to just the new warehouse once we felt confident. I presented the decision to the stakeholders with strong reassurances.

Once the exterior buildings were roughed in at the new location, the team and I were on-site twelve to fifteen hours a day. Many of us commuted over an hour each night and did it all over again the next morning. Weekends disappeared. Soon, it was time to put the parallel warehouses into motion. We made just enough progress to get our hopes up. But then we hit a wall. The dual warehouse setup was working in theory, but there was a minor problem: we lost visibility of our inventory. In a short time, we had an unmanageable mess on our hands.

Our only choice? Move all the inventory into the new warehouse and go live on the new system without the backup plan. I dreaded telling the stakeholders. As the project director, I would be taking away a safety net I had assured them would be there. On one hand, we were far enough along that a complete breakdown of the system seemed unlikely. On the other hand, the chance of the parallel warehouse not working had also seemed unlikely.

I remember watching the clock before starting the videoconference to tell my superiors. My mouth was dry, and my hands were sweaty. I was grateful and surprised when they took the news in stride; however, the burden wasn't completely lifted. Our technical defeat was excusable, but it couldn't flow through to our customers. The stakeholders' confidence in me wasn't destroyed, but a question mark had replaced the period, and I didn't like that. Those moments when we feel the chink in our armor are the most painful.

I think I literally held my breath when we cut everything over to the new distribution center. If you've ever implemented systems or managed a construction project, you know no matter how much planning and testing you do, you simply cannot plan for every scenario. It didn't take long for the system to generate error messages. After practically living on-site in a freezing warehouse shell for months, we were all frustrated, and the most recent flop with the parallel warehouses lingered. The words *error* and *failure* swirled dangerously close to each other. Then Jeff, my supply chain manager, said, "We just put something incredibly powerful into motion. The system is just telling us how to make it better."[5] He also mentioned that none of the error messages would delay or stop shipments. We should be celebrating!

Jeff was right, and his reframe was just what we needed. There's a quote that's been attributed to lots of different people, so the source is unknown, but the sentiment is solid: "The only people who never make mistakes are the people who never do anything." The error messages were proof we had done something. We created something colossal from scratch. Our new robotic system was fast, efficient, and wildly innovative. It would carry the company far into the future.

We started looking at every error as feedback to help us fine-tune the machine, seeing them as flags waving over areas that needed finishing touches. Each tune-up took the system a step closer to being its best version, and that, dear leader, is the gift of failure.

SACRED WORK

There are so many lessons to be learned from failures, but those involving our relationships with other people have the potential to be the most important. To move forward requires us to approach conversations and situations with humility. Maybe you've made a mistake with an employee, like I did with Amanda. Don't despair. Instead, carry your humility forward into every conversation with your employee. Reset the relationship by being honest about your mistake and how you'll lead differently from now on.

As I talked with my friend Jessica about these failure resets, she commented how this approach echoes the rhythm of confession and repentance God sets before us. We acknowledge our sin for what it is, turn away from it, and can then reset our course.

Romans 3:23–24 tells us we all fall short of the glory of God and are justified freely by His grace. Because we know God has forgiven us of every sin, we come to Him with our failures and mistakes and confess them for what they are—holy shortcomings. Then we can turn away from our sin and back toward God. Repentance acknowledges where we've gone off-course and is a conscious decision to claim God's forgiveness and His grace, knowing He will set us back on a solid path.

When you feel like quitting or not risking anything at all, remember God's power is working within you and through you for His glory. Misjudgments at work, home, or in any area of our lives are bound to happen. We make a hasty decision or a poor one. Our priorities get jumbled up, and our relationships get off balance. We disappoint our family, friends, coworkers, or boss. When this happens, we can grieve the consequences, but we don't have to camp out there.

God doesn't want to pin us down in punishment. Instead, He wants us to learn, grow, and draw closer to Him. He wants us to fail forward. Remember, God is more about reclaiming and redeeming than keeping score.

My prayer for you: Father, thank You for Your mercy and grace and how You grow us through our fumbles and failures. I pray for the woman reading these words, Father. In the same way You extend grace to us, I pray she would extend grace to herself. Help her learn from what has happened and remember that she isn't weaker because of it; she is stronger. Remove the sting of this mistake or failure, Father, and replace it with Your acceptance and love. Thank You for Your faithfulness and Your perfect example.

11

When You and Your Boss Disagree

My dear brothers and sisters, take note of this: Everyone should be quick
to listen, slow to speak and slow to become angry, because human anger
does not produce the righteousness that God desires.

JAMES 1:19–20

Leaders aren't in the habit of keeping ideas to themselves. You
didn't get promoted to leadership because you're afraid to speak
up or think independently. But what if the person you're challenging
has the power to hurt your career or even fire you? Conflict with your
boss isn't the same as conflict with other people in your organization.

When you disagree with your superior, you're positioning yourself
against the person who can affect your current and future position.
If fear shows up, it can feel easier to agree—even if you don't. Shrinking back or consistently complying isn't sustainable long-term, and
this choice also prevents you from having an authentic relationship.

So what do you do? How do you know when it's worth saying
something? Do you only disagree with deal-breaker issues? How
do you know when a disagreement is healthy and professional and
when it's not? What's the best approach?

These are tough questions, but let me assure you: you've got this because God's got you! He knew about the argument or difference of opinion you'd have with your boss before you ever picked up this book. His Word generously gives us wisdom on this topic, and He divinely orchestrated a collection of experiences from leaders, just like you, to help you. God has a lot of experience in brokering peace, so keep an expectant heart. He is with you!

WORKPLACE DISAGREEMENTS: NORMAL AND EXPECTED

First, understand that leaders and the people they report to will naturally disagree on minor and major issues. Healthy workplaces make it safe for employees to disagree with their higher-ups. Different perspectives, insights, and ideas are welcome within healthy teams and so is open and honest communication. To foster reciprocal and effective conversations with your boss, there are certain guidelines you'll want to follow.

If a disagreement happens over conflicting ideas or viewpoints, leadership author Catherine Gates suggests this: "Take the time to understand your boss and find out what they're thinking. Ask questions. What are their concerns? Where is the disconnect between your perception and theirs? You need to try to understand where they're coming from."[1] Catherine and I came up with these additional tips:

- Pray for a sincere desire to understand their viewpoint and the ability to communicate yours.
- Ask yourself key questions like these: Have I latched onto a certain outcome? What am I failing to convey? What questions can I ask to increase understanding?
- Put your agenda aside and remember your perspective isn't the only one.

- Listen. Don't attack their position or defend yours. Sit with what your boss is telling you.
- After the conversation, give yourself time to process everything.[2]

Just as you don't want to habitually agree with everything your superior says, you also don't want to do the opposite. I once worked for someone whose leadership and management practices differed greatly from mine, and my first reaction was typically pushback. One night I was reading through my sent emails, looking for a specific one. After reading several messages I had sent my boss, I was appalled—at myself! My behavior was borderline insubordinate. I wasn't just disagreeing; I was being disagreeable. God, in His mercy, brought this to my attention, and I corrected my course.

In my case, I needed to take a hard look at myself and my motivations. I didn't have to always agree with my supervisor, but in order to maintain professionalism and integrity as a follower of Christ, I needed to change my behavior. Constantly disagreeing, no matter the topic, wasn't acceptable.

Agreeing and disagreeing can and should happen naturally. If you notice you're most often doing one or the other, there is probably a deeper issue that needs to be addressed.

WHEN YOUR VALUES ARE COMPROMISED

Disagreements with the person in charge won't always fall into the "normal and expected" category. What should you do when your supervisor repeatedly takes credit for your work or asks you to do something that goes against your values? How can you stand firm in your faith and integrity without jeopardizing your career or relationship with your boss? The hard answer is sometimes you can't.

Your moral compass may point you opposite of where your boss wants you or send you on a new career path at a different company.

As a young professional, my values were tested when "Sandra," my supervisor, asked me to participate in coaching sessions with her. She explained that a consultant would coach us on how to use our personality differences as strengths, which would help us work together more effectively. Sandra and I both had strong personalities and our disagreements sometimes leaned toward friction, so this idea seemed practical, and I agreed to the coaching.

Later that night, I wrote in my prayer journal about my disappointment.

Before we started our first session, Sandra and the consultant had a brief personal conversation about their families. They clearly already knew each other, which seemed odd, but I put my concerns aside. The session started, and I immediately went on high alert because the consultant used new-age terms like "channeling your inner spirit" and "manifesting positivity." At the end of the session, she gave me her business card, and I saw that her title was "shaman." There was no way I would agree to continue coaching with a shaman, and I dreaded having this conversation with Sandra.

Later that night, I wrote in my prayer journal about my disappointment. I knew God wanted me in this position, at this specific company, but I wasn't sure how Sandra would handle my refusal to continue with the coaching program. Flipping back through the pages of my journal, I noticed a verse I'd written and highlighted a few weeks earlier: "Get wisdom, get understanding; do not forget my words or turn away from them. Do not forsake wisdom, and she will protect you; love her, and she will watch over you" (Prov. 4:5–6). God reminded me that because my allegiance was to Him, my future was secure in Him. I prayerfully claimed His promises and by morning, I knew what to do.

The next day, I told Sandra I couldn't agree to any more sessions with the consultant, and I told her why. I gave her a list of consultants and said I'd be willing to try again with anyone on the list. She argued in defense of the shaman, but I wouldn't back down. After telling me how complicated I'd made everything, she agreed to look at the list. I left not knowing how this conversation might affect my future with the company, but nothing further happened. After a few months, I followed up with Sandra about the coaching, and she said we were doing fine and didn't need it. I wasn't in complete agreement, but the Holy Spirit closed my mouth, and the situation rested.

In this case, I disagreed with my boss because what she wanted me to do compromised my values, and I wasn't willing to budge. As Christians, our faith forms our values, and when we're asked to do something that contradicts our faith, we can't go along. You'll inevitably work with people who have different values and believe differently than you do. Because *your* values represent *your* individual beliefs, you're the one who has to stand up for and set boundaries around them.

SIX QUESTIONS TO HELP YOU
EVALUATE YOUR PERSPECTIVE

Not every disagreement will challenge your values. When standard disputes happen, there are six questions you can ask to help you decide if your objections are well-founded. Record your answers, so when you're finished, you'll have an outline to help you decide if you want to continue pushing your viewpoint or if you need to back down.

1. **What exactly is your boss asking you to do?** Are you sure you understand what's being asked of you? Is the person in charge asking you to do something that goes against your

values? Is it morally wrong? Does it compromise your beliefs? Or was there a misunderstanding between what your
boss asked and what you perceived?

2. **Why do you object?** What's at the heart of your unwilling-
ness to agree? Conduct an honest self-assessment where
you concretely identify the reason behind your objection.
Is your objection centered on Christ? Is it a difference of
opinion or something deeper?

3. **What's your relationship like with your boss?** Would
you categorize it as healthy and stable? New and tenuous?
Burdened with baggage? Evaluate how well you know your
boss, how long you've known each other, and the strength
of your relationship. The quality of your relationship plays
an important role in weathering disagreements.

4. **How often do you disagree with your boss, and what
about?** Write the last three to five times you and your superior were on different sides of an issue. Note the issue and
the approximate date. How frequently does this happen? Are
the issues big or small? Is there a pattern related to the topic?

5. **How do you typically voice your disagreement?** The way
you express or communicate when you disagree affects your
relationship, as well as the outcome. Do you disagree in an
agreeable way? Record everything you remember about the
most recent disagreement and then evaluate how you handled
it. If possible, ask an unbiased third party for feedback on how
you've dealt with disagreements in the past. What are your
blind spots, and what do you need to improve on personally?

6. **Are you strategic with the time and place?** If you disagree with your supervisor in front of other people, you've
set yourself up for failure. Disagreeing in private decreases
the chance they'll respond defensively. The same goes for

arguing in the heat of the moment. Instead, thoughtfully and constructively present your points when you and your supervisor are in the best frame of mind. Refer to your answers in number four above and jot down where and when the disagreements took place. Then look for patterns you may need to change.

Answering these questions helps you step out of your emotions. Your brain changes from reactive to evaluative, which enables you to make your next decision carefully: to pursue or rescind your objection.

HOW TO HANDLE DISAGREEMENTS: THREE TYPICAL SCENARIOS

There are certain scenarios that lend themselves to disagreements between you and the person you report to. You are human beings and each have hot-buttons, personality quirks, and different communication styles. When these individual idiosyncrasies mix with specific circumstances, the perfect storm begins to brew. Knowing potential pitfalls now can help you prevent them or manage their outcomes in a positive way. When the following conditions exist, a disagreement with your leader is more likely to happen:

Scenario One: **You get a new boss, and you really liked your previous one.** When a new leader arrives on the scene, you're forced to deal with a new person and all the changes they begin to make. You were comfortable with how your previous supervisor communicated, operated within the organization, and interacted with you. Your old supervisor probably implemented strategies and projects you spearheaded and are still attached to. Your new supervisor may change how often they meet with you, how they handle company-wide meetings, or the organization's priorities. You may be tempted to resist, disagree, and protest.

Solution: In a word, don't. Don't resist, disagree, and protest—at least, not at first. *Whatever* your supervisor's approach, it likely exists because it worked somewhere else. Take the time to learn from them and understand their reasoning. What they're proposing may be a positive change your company benefits from. If you don't give them a chance, you won't know. As a leader, it's also your responsibility to help them integrate successfully into the company. Put aside what you're used to and focus on helping them. Build a relationship (and credibility) before offering feedback.

Scenario Two: **The stakes are high and so are stress levels.** In crisis situations, disagreements can quickly spin out of control: companies suffer from high turnover that negatively impacts the bottom line. Leaders have to manage talent shortages, remote work challenges, and the emergence of technologies like artificial intelligence. Others must make rapid decisions about how to respond to economic changes and supply chain dilemmas. Your ideas about how to handle these situations may differ from what your superior has in mind. You may even think their solution has a high possibility of failure, and you don't want to see that happen.

Solution: In high-stress scenarios, the best way to be an effective advocate for the company is to be a powerful advocate for your boss. Approach your differences from a place of trust and respect. Be calm and stay focused on solutions, regardless of who gets credit. Clearly explain the outcomes of your ideas and how they will benefit those affected and the company. If you don't understand their reasoning or what's being proposed, ask questions to clarify before you disagree. High-pressure situations call for fast, sound decisions, and senseless disagreements can get in the way.

Scenario Three: **You have conflicting personalities.** If you're an introvert like me, you don't enjoy small talk or disclosing personal information to someone you don't know. When your superior is the opposite, you may clam up or dread the forced socializing before every one-on-one. If you're an extrovert with an introvert for a supervisor, you may want more calls or in-person interactions while they prefer email and chat. Over time, these types of differences can create or exacerbate disagreements.

Solution: Take a step back and ask yourself if the two of you are disagreeing about an actual issue. Personality differences make it seem as if two people disagree when they really don't. Rather, their communication styles are simply different, and they aren't understanding one another. Clarify your supervisor's position by asking for it outright or paraphrasing it back. Be mindful of their personality when presenting your viewpoint. If they're analytical, use numbers and data. If they're visionary, skip the details. Adjust your approach and find common ground. The faster you're able to understand how personality differences affect your ability to work together, the less strain you'll place on your relationship. You won't inadvertently create conflict, and when a disagreement comes up, you'll be prepared to handle it.

DISAGREEING WITH YOUR BOSS
CAN BE A GOOD THING

As a leader, your ability to come up with innovative ideas and solutions has served you well. What you have to offer has already benefited the company, which is why you were hired or promoted in the first place. So don't be fearful about disagreeing; conflict can be a catalyst for change! Disagreements don't have to be detrimental and can actually contribute to stronger relationships.

Staci Diffendaffer is a real estate investor and the author of *Unconditioned Love: Healing Hearts and Minds in a Time of Conflict and Division*. Years before she started her own business, she was a contract employee. Her manager scheduled a meeting thirty minutes after the workday ended. Since she was a contract employee, Staci didn't get paid for her wait time. Her manager didn't show up for the meeting, and forty-five minutes later, Staci left. She attempted to reach her manager several times but never received a response.

That night, Staci emailed her manager. She wanted to address what had happened and prevent it from happening again. "I started by saying I valued her as a person and the person in charge. Then I explained that I waited for one hour and fifteen minutes without pay. I told her my time was just as important as hers and asked her to respect me by respecting my time."[3] Staci concluded the email by setting boundaries for future meetings. The next day, Staci's manager apologized for not showing up or communicating. After this incident, meetings happened based on Staci's terms. The manager respected her for speaking up and even lovingly nicknamed her "the Lioness."[4]

As with Staci's manager, most employers want their leaders to be assertive and independent thinkers. They value employees who bring constructive feedback and new suggestions into the business.

Rather than shying away from conversations where you don't agree, be strategic and thoughtful about how and when you disagree. Invest time in thinking through your approach and how to communicate it. There's a strong possibility that, like Staci, you'll gain more respect from your superior and better results for the company.

SACRED WORK

For the LORD gives wisdom; from his mouth come knowledge and understanding. He holds success in store for the upright, he is a shield to those whose walk is blameless, for he guards the course of the just and protects the way of his faithful ones.

PROVERBS 2:6–8

Proverbs teaches us how God's wisdom, along with godly boundaries, can show us how to approach disagreements with our bosses. In Proverbs 2:6, we're reminded that wisdom comes from God. I love that this reminder is both a comfort and a caution. If we aren't sure when or how we should speak up, or if we should speak up at all, God tells us we don't have to worry! He will give us what we need. We may not know the best timing or the best words, but what a comfort to remember—He knows. When we embrace this truth, we gain confidence and peace.

This same verse serves as a caution against pride. If we don't stop to consider our boss's perspective or what God would have us do, we're letting pride rob us of the best possible outcome. The conflicts I've faced using my own wisdom, and not God's, left me uneasy and regretful. Proverbs 2:6b says, "From his mouth come knowledge and understanding." In the Hebrew language, the meaning behind the words *knowledge* and *understanding* includes perception, skill,[5] intelligence, discretion, insight, and skillfulness.[6] God is offering to give us so much! Look at the list again, and imagine facing a disagreement with your boss, knowing that you have access to all these attributes.

Proverbs 2:7 says, "He holds success in store for the upright, he is a shield to those whose walk is blameless." The words *upright* and *blameless*, meaning marked by integrity, help us understand godly boundaries. I talked earlier about being disagreeable with one of my bosses and how God opened my eyes to my sinful behavior. Being rebellious and disrespectful removed God's wisdom and shield from me because I wasn't walking within the boundaries of obedience. I wasn't being upright, blameless, or walking in integrity, so I caused undue stress between me and my boss. He could have written me up for insubordination. In the other situation I shared about the disagreement over a shaman, I confidently followed God's lead, and His path led to peace. "He guards the course of the just and protects the way of his faithful ones" (v. 8).

In addition to being wise, God loves you! He cares about your company, your boss, and how you interact with one another. When you object to something your boss says or does, remember that God longs to be included and to provide what you need.

My prayer for you: Father, I pray for the leader reading these words. There's a lot of tension and pressure involved when we disagree with our bosses. Help her accept the courage, calm, and confidence You promise through Your wisdom. Grant her discernment, so she sees the situation through Your eyes. I pray You would guide her words and her heart. I pray, too, for her boss, that this person would be receptive, wise, and fair. We lift up the situation and the outcome to You, Father. Thank You for Your promises and the gift of wisdom that comes from You.

12

When You're Betrayed at Work

... forgiving each other, just as in Christ God forgave you.

EPHESIANS 4:32

You're juggling numerous responsibilities and forging ahead with your team when, out of nowhere, someone breaches your trust. A teammate gossips about you. A trusted coworker takes your idea and runs with it. A colleague makes a mistake but lets you take the fall. A workplace friend and peer supports you in private but doesn't back you in public. Or worse yet, a person who professes the same faith moves against you deliberately.

None of these examples are easy to manage, but the last one is particularly hard. The pain of duplicity seems to double if the offending person is a Christian. A breach of trust in the workplace is harmful and hurtful, and when someone from your faith community is responsible, the hurt travels deeper. Christians have certain principles they expect people of their faith to uphold.

When these principles aren't followed, you're disappointed and offended. You value integrity and honest relationships, so the situation throws you off-kilter. The projects you're working on fade into the background, and the ugliness of what feels like a double-cross comes into sharp focus.

How should you respond when a peer deceives you or a coworker violates your trust? How can you forgive and move on? What can you do to restore relationships? Workplace dynamics are complex. People have varying motivations and reasons they do or say things to hurt you. How you choose to respond to the offense affects how others view your leadership and who you are as a follower of Christ. This is a heavy responsibility to carry, but one you don't bear alone. Forgiveness isn't dependent on the other person; it's a process you and God handle together. You're equipped for it because of what He's done and who you are in Him.

The issue of workplace betrayal and the process of forgiveness are familiar to me and other Christian leaders I know. When you read our stories, you'll discover constructive ways to manage the disappointment of broken trust without letting it defeat you professionally or spiritually. I'll also share steps you can take after trust is broken to secure the best possible outcome.

TWO TYPES OF WORKPLACE BETRAYAL

Two main types of betrayal in the workplace are oversight and offense. Knowing which type you're dealing with provides insight and helps you process what at first may feel like backstabbing or disloyalty. Then you can reflect on what happened in a more objective way, and at that point, you're better able to assess your feelings and respond. The process gives you space to analyze what happened and what your next steps will be.

Type 1—**Oversight:** When an oversight happens, the person who committed it didn't have malicious intentions. Dr. Dennis Reina, founder of the Reina Trust Building Institute, says, "About 85 percent of workplace betrayal—a breach of trust or the perception of that breach—is unintended."[1] Betrayal by oversight is minor and easier to recover from than intentional betrayals.

Here's an example: You invest time mentoring your administrative assistant. You give her a significant raise and negotiate a title change for her, which your boss was reluctant to agree to. A couple of weeks later, your assistant submits her notice. You're disappointed and upset because you spent time and effort helping her advance. She didn't tell you about looking for another job or leaving. Instead, she resigned, leaving you in a lurch with one short week to find a replacement. What will your boss say? You just lobbied for the title change!

The administrative assistant didn't set out to harm your career, yet she seems disloyal. You devoted time and resources to her professional growth and expected her to be equally committed to her job and you. The reality, however, is that you weren't doing her a favor: you were doing your job. As a leader and talent manager, you help people grow and make sure they're paid fairly. You did your job, and your assistant did hers. She earned her raise and title change. Perhaps what you're upset about is what you perceive as a lack of loyalty. You also don't look forward to what your boss will say. In both cases, pride is a factor. I share these reflections because they're my own. This example is a story that happened to me.

Instead of asking my assistant, I assumed her work priorities were the same as mine.

When I talked to my administrative assistant, she explained that an opportunity opened up for her closer to home, with the same pay but a more flexible schedule. She was a single mom, so these job perks were ideal for her. She didn't tell me sooner because she felt bad about how much I'd invested in her, so she put off the conversation. I told her I was disappointed, but I now understood her decision.

Later, I realized that pay and job security were important to me when I was a single mom, so instead of asking my assistant, I assumed her work priorities were the same as mine. Had I asked her, perhaps I could have pursued different options for her. I also recognized how my personal pride was impacting the situation. It was prideful to expect an employee to put her loyalty to me above everything else, and it was my pride that didn't want to face my boss again after fighting so hard to prove my assistant's worth. I needed a dose of humility, and God used that situation to give it to me.

How to respond: A betrayal by oversight doesn't have long-lasting repercussions, and it's the easiest type of offense to recover from. A person may handle a situation in a disappointing way, but their intentions probably weren't malicious. When this type of offense happens, first be honest with yourself about why you feel betrayed. Later, have a conversation to discover the other person's perspective and learn from what happened. This also gives you a chance for closure by sharing how the situation made you feel. You may have been embarrassed, devalued, or even confused. Finally, decide to make changes based on what you learned. What is within your power to do so this type of oversight doesn't happen again? Use what happened as a catalyst for improvement.

Your experience with oversight may differ from mine. Here are some other common examples of oversight in the workplace. Are any of these familiar?

> a colleague fails to invite you to a strategy meeting
>
> an employee forgets to run a critical report for an important meeting
>
> a peer makes a customer commitment that compromises your department

your co-manager misses a key deadline on an extensive project

These oversights are unintentional, but the consequences can create powerful emotions and reactions. Be honest with yourself about the feelings you're experiencing, talk to the other person about what happened, and then learn from it.

Type 2—**Offense:** An offense happens when someone *knowingly* harms or offends you. You're blindsided by what they said or did, and you're wondering if trust is repairable. The closer your relationship, the more painful the injury. I'll share two women's stories of offenses and their responses. Even though their situations are different, there's a common pattern to their responses:

Pause ———⟶ Process ———⟶ Confront ———⟶ Forgive ———⟶ Heal

Notice as you read each story how God fills the gaps between each step of the process. Whether through prayer, Scripture, or a mentor—God's presence ushers in forgiveness.

Example 1: "Kelly" is a chief marketing officer in the healthcare industry. She was excited when "Angie," a friend from church, was hired at her company. Angie worked in a different department, but Kelly helped her get settled at the company, and they met for lunch often. Two months following Angie's employment, Kelly was in the restroom when she heard two women enter. One started talking negatively about Kelly. "How'd she get promoted so quickly? It definitely wasn't because she's good at her job!" Kelly didn't recognize the woman's voice, but when the second woman chimed in and agreed, Kelly immediately recognized Angie's voice. After waiting for the two women to leave, Kelly returned to her office.[2]

Kelly's response: I marched back to my office and came to terms with what I'd overheard. Though I was terribly upset, I wouldn't allow the conversation to affect my work. I put the brakes on and decided to process what had happened later. While driving home, I prayed and told God how I felt about Angie agreeing with the person who was gossiping about me. Friends should defend one another, and her behavior made me think she didn't care about our friendship.

Ranting or not, prayer was still the best place for me to start. Angie's words wounded me, and the human side of me wanted to hurt her by telling someone what she did or confronting her in anger. After praying, I was still upset, but the urge to lash out was gone. God helped me get my head and heart in the right place. In the book of Matthew, the Bible says to keep offenses between you and the other person, so I didn't talk about what happened to anyone else (see Matt. 18:15). I continued to pray and put the incident on pause until I was at peace about confronting Angie.

I asked her to coffee the weekend after and told her how I felt about what happened. In tears, she apologized. She didn't defend me because she was trying so hard to fit in. What she said resonated with me. I thought of times I'd done something similar—stayed quiet when I should have spoken up. We'd been friends for years, so I chose to forgive and reinvest trust. We survived that season, and we're still friends to this day.[3]

Example 2: I asked Erica, the founder of Faith & Gather, if she'd ever dealt with a workplace betrayal. She did have a story but said she had almost forgotten it because God had helped her heal and move past it. I'm glad she didn't forget it because her story reminds us that forgiveness doesn't require reconciliation. We can forgive, even if we don't resume the same relationship afterward.

An organization experimenting with a new position hired Erica as an hourly employee. The position demanded a lot of hours, so they regularly paid her overtime. During Erica's second year, leadership moved her from hourly to salary. She was concerned her pay would decrease, though the workload would remain unchanged. Without knowing her concerns, her boss negotiated a salary consistent with what she had made the year before. The salary was acceptable, but Erica was still apprehensive. She wasn't sure if the hours and responsibilities would increase as well. The amount was fair, but Erica wanted to be sure she could cover her living expenses. Receiving a set amount, regardless of the hours worked, was a big change for her.

Shortly after, a partner at the company asked Erica her thoughts about switching to salary. As a partner, he knew about the change and budget details, and his concern seemed genuine, so Erica was honest about her apprehension. The next thing she knew, Erica was called into her boss's office. He was furious. The partner had told him that Erica asked for more money and was unhappy with her salary. Erica felt stabbed in the back and foolish because the partner had a reputation for being untrustworthy and she had trusted him.

> Forgiveness did not, however, include letting her guard down. She was cautious with what she said around him.

The partner betrayed Erica, and her boss initially believed Erica had betrayed him. After several tough, intense conversations, Erica and her boss found common ground. Her boss knew the partner's reputation, so he understood what happened. What followed was an awkward confrontation with Erica, her boss, and the partner, who apologized.

Erica accepted his apology and remained cordial with him, but she didn't trust him. Erica explains that we can be aware of ulterior motives without compromising kindness and respect. She recognized that God expected her to care for and respect the partner. The more she focused on caring and respecting, the more she healed and forgave. Forgiveness did not, however, include letting her guard down. She was cautious with what she said around him and kept their interactions to a minimum.[4]

Conclusion: Kelly and Erica experienced different betrayals and their outcomes were different too. But there were similarities in how they responded—namely, forgiveness. As you saw with Erica, forgiving someone doesn't mean you resume the same relationship you had before the betrayal. Instead, it means getting your heart right with God and letting go of bitterness and resentment. Even if you can't trust the other person, you can trust God. You can nurture forgiveness or you can nurture resentment; you can't nurture both.

Responding to Offense: Ten Key Steps

Workplace betrayals may be intentional or unintentional and can cover a wide spectrum of hurt. Every scenario is different depending on relationships, workplace dynamics, and what's at stake. Here are ten steps you can take to help you secure the best possible outcome after a betrayal happens:

1. Don't act on your anger or frustration.
2. Pause and step away from the situation—physically and emotionally.
3. Vent to God first.
4. Turn to the Bible for guidance. I recommend starting with Matthew 6:5–15 and 1 John 1:5–10.
5. Seek wise counsel.
6. Remain professional in your interactions with the other person.
7. Recognize your part in the offense.

8. Approach the person from a place of humility, honor, and love.

9. Understand that forgiveness may not result in reconciliation.

10. Remember that forgiveness is between you and God and is possible because of God.

Getting to the Bottom of a Betrayal: A Practical Exercise

Betrayal destabilizes you because it's painful and unexpected. One constructive way to process an initial offense is to journal answers to questions, which allows you to explore and process what happened. As you answer the questions, you take all your jumbled thoughts and disruptive emotions and put them on paper. Even if you never share what you write with another person, you're acknowledging and accepting your feelings, which is an important first step toward healing.

Use these questions to guide you through the journaling process so you can navigate the pain of what happened. Your answers can also be a helpful reference later if you choose to speak with a mentor or friend for counsel:

1. What did the person do or say?
2. Why do I think this person betrayed me?
3. What emotions did I feel right after? How do I feel now?
4. Have I ever done something similar to someone else? What happened? Why did I do what I did?
5. How close am I to this person? How long have we worked together? What difficulties have we been through together?
6. Has this person ever hurt me before? Have I ever hurt them?
7. How do I feel about forgiveness right now?
8. How can I pray for this person? How can I pray for our relationship?

9. What stories or verses from the Bible apply to what happened?
10. What is God teaching me? What can I do differently next time?
11. What do I hope happens next? How can God help me move forward?

Important Takeaway

Whether intentional or not, betrayal in the workplace can leave us angry, frustrated, and even heartbroken. God doesn't expect us to forget about it or pretend it never happened, but He does want us to work through it and include Him in the process.

SACRED WORK

When someone at work breaks our trust, that breach isn't easy to recover from, especially if that person shares our faith. Their hurtful actions may make our jobs more difficult, discredit us, or prevent us from getting a promotion or raise. We have to address the damage done and the recovery plan. We need to maintain professionalism and composure while allowing God to lead us to forgiveness. It may seem impossible, but it isn't—unless we try to do it alone.

I once sat on a panel interviewing candidates for a management position. While the finalist and I were at lunch, she asked me about local churches. In the weeks after my company hired her, she often brought up faith-related topics when we interacted. I was excited to have a peer who was a Christian, especially one whose department worked closely with mine.

A couple of months later, I came into the conference room as the manager and one of the higher ups were leaving. I sat down and saw papers they'd left behind on the table. The top paper was a proposal by the manager with an organizational chart showing my position crossed out and the new hire's name in my place. With a quick glance, I understood her goal: to merge our departments and displace my position. I confronted her, and she said she was simply brainstorming with my boss. I didn't believe her, and we didn't resolve our differences. This incident was the first of several. Over and over, God prompted me to approach confrontations with humility and honor. I reluctantly agreed and constantly wrestled with forgiveness until a year later, when she resigned.

Matthew 18:21–22 is a familiar passage: "Then Peter came to Jesus and asked, 'Lord, how many times shall I forgive my brother or sister who sins against me? Up to seven times?' Jesus answered, 'I tell you, not seven times, but seventy-seven times.'" These numbers add up to an attitude of forgiveness. Jesus is saying we need to forgive more than we can measure and more than we can do on our own. When I've sat in the wreckage of betrayal, Jesus has faithfully shown up. He gently reminds me of how I've hurt others, and the Holy Spirit reminds me that focusing on someone else's hypocrisy blinds me to the hypocrisy in myself. The same grace, love, and forgiveness that flows across my offenses also flows through to my offender.

Scripture reminds us that not only is forgiveness possible, but it's also a matter of obedience. God commands us to forgive. "Bear with each other and forgive one another if any of you has a grievance against someone. Forgive as the Lord forgave you" (Col. 3:13). What if God gave us this command because He knows what unforgiveness does to our hearts? Unforgiveness cultivates rivalry, hostility, bitterness, and even hatred. These feelings have no place in a heart created in God's image, a heart that is loved and forgiven by Him. And these are feelings God has *chosen* not to have toward us when He *chose* to forgive us. He had every right to be hostile toward our sin, but His love chose mercy over judgment—and that's the model He wants for us too. When we choose to surrender these feelings, we can lead and forgive as holy and wholly healed people.

13

When You're Passed Over for a Promotion

I believe nothing that happens to me is without meaning . . . As I see it,
I'm here for some purpose, and I only hope I may fulfill it.[1]

DIETRICH BONHOEFFER, THEOLOGIAN AND AUTHOR

Being rejected for a promotion is painful and can shake a leader's confidence, yet it's possible to take losses without being defeated. The outcome of a rejection feels like failure, but it can also become a powerful catalyst for reflection, growth, and change. In other chapters, we've looked at challenges women face because gender parity is still a work in progress. There are unfair situations where women should get promoted but don't; in this chapter, we'll focus on outcomes more than reasons. We'll explore ways to regroup when a promotion doesn't happen and learn how to discover God's ideas about what's next.

God uses the rejections we experience at work to move us forward in our careers, lives, and faith. We can't change the fact that we were passed over, but we can change how we respond. And even though we may have felt defeated in the moment, we have the ability to change the outcome. Rejections don't get the final say!

NO C-SUITE FOR ME

There's a theme to how God transforms me. He understands my inner workings and how stubborn and obsessive I can be, so He lets me have my way. He lets me run with whatever idol I've picked up until not only is it too heavy to carry, but it also makes me spiritually sick. I don't just drop it; I throw it. I usually go big, so my fall is equally hard, and the lesson learned in the aftermath is long-lasting. God knows all this, so when I ignored His prompting to get on a different career track, He gave me the jolt I needed and, as I'll share with you, it was one I couldn't ignore.

The Holy Spirit had clearly shown me that the next step in my career would not be up the corporate ladder. For a few years, I had dreamed of starting my own business as a freelance writer. I prayed, talked to friends and mentors, journaled, and did lots of research. I made plans and spreadsheets, and God spoke into all my efforts with a resounding yes. Yet, I stayed put.

Fear kept me rooted when I should have moved forward in faith. I kept pushing to meet my corporate goals and get the next project under my belt. I knew I wasn't where God wanted me, but I couldn't step off the fast track. Everything changed when I was passed over for a C-suite position.

This promotion, I told myself, was the natural next step in my career progression. If you're picturing Jonah running in the opposite direction God sends him, you're spot on. Right before my interview, I needed emergency surgery, so with the panel's full support I postponed the interview. After a successful surgery, I spent three days in the hospital and went home. A friend at headquarters called me while I was resting and said a different candidate had been interviewed and hired while I was in surgery. I was floored and flooded with an onslaught of emotions: shock, anger, disappointment, and hurt.

Working from home to recuperate gave me several weeks to process what happened. Having that reflection time was priceless. I sought God every way I knew how: praying, reading His Word, and talking to people with godly counsel. I asked business and spiritual mentors what they thought was happening,

I couldn't control what happened then, but I could control what happened next.

and I forced myself to listen. God used that time to teach me more about Him, myself, and the decisions I was making in my career. It was a grueling, painful season, but I learned a few key things:

My job had become an idol. God had given me the job to provide for me and my daughter when I was a single parent. I had taken that gift and allowed it to take over my life.

Pride and fear were dictating my career decisions. People who loved me asked painful, revealing questions: Did you really want the job, or were you just taking the next step because you're competitive and an overachiever? You know God is calling you to write. Why aren't you pursuing that? What are you afraid of?

Forgiveness was needed. God forgave me and called me to let go of the bitterness and resentment I carried toward others, as well as the disappointment and shame I felt toward myself. My eyes were opened to how empty my professional pursuits had become. I was running for a finish line I had created, one that was completely off course. God had blessed me, and I had dishonored that blessing.

God wastes nothing. He uses every misstep, rejection, or failure to move us closer to our calling and deeper into a relationship with Him. This experience opened my eyes and helped me embrace a new level of surrendering my will to His.

Through this situation, God propelled me into the career change He had been calling me to make for two years. During those two years, I had a million excuses for not transitioning, which all came down to trust. Your situation may be similar, or it may be wildly different, but there is one part of our stories I know is identical: I couldn't control what happened then, but I could control what happened next. The same was true for my friend "Tammy," whose story you'll read next, and the same is true for you.

WHEN GETTING PASSED OVER FEELS PERSONAL

Tammy is the CEO of a consumer electronics company that began as her family's small business decades ago. She started working for the company at an early age, learning every part of the trade. Her two older brothers had no interest in it, but Tammy's father, Henry, provided them with high-level opportunities as the company grew. He never extended these offers to her. Eventually, her brothers left to pursue other careers, but she stayed and had lots of conversations with her dad about marketing strategies and the company's future. She had an aptitude for business, and he implemented many of her ideas.

A leadership opportunity opened up, and Henry offered it to his nephew, someone with no industry experience. The nephew left soon after and wasn't replaced. Tammy felt frustrated as she watched Henry pursue other people to fill positions she was qualified for and wanted. Out of respect, she chose not to say anything. I asked her why she stayed, and she said, "I literally grew up in the company, and even though I didn't have a title or get any credit, my work and ideas helped make it successful. I had a vision I wouldn't give up on."[2] She kept managing multiple roles without a formal title until her father offered her the position of COO with the request that she fix one of the product lines that was failing. Tammy accepted.

Sales skyrocketed, and she watched her aging father get completely overwhelmed and taken advantage of by people in the industry. She asked him about taking on more responsibilities so she could be more helpful. Through this conversation, Henry agreed his role in the company had grown beyond him. He said he would appoint his grandson, a recent college graduate, as temporary CEO.

Tammy was stunned and hurt but persuaded her father not to act on this idea. Henry's health declined shortly after, and he turned the business over to her. She wouldn't say this herself, but I know the company is thriving today under her leadership. I asked her what advice she had for women who have experienced what feels like deeply personal rejection in their careers. Here are my thoughts about what she shared:

Be kind to yourself. A rejection may have nothing to do with you and more to do with the interviewer. There are influences and biases you aren't aware of, so try not to take the outcome personally. Take time to decide if you want to stay with the company, and if you do, use what you learned from the experience to work on your future. Remember that progress takes time, so set reasonable goals and expectations. If you're sure of what you want, don't receive the rejection as "never," but view it as "not yet."

Look for what the experience can teach you. Tammy worked in a male-led industry, and what happened in her family business prepared her to navigate it. Though being overlooked many times was painful, the experience taught her resilience and perseverance. It also made her more empathetic and aware as a leader. Her dad passed away right after she became CEO, so she stepped into new responsibilities with little guidance or direction. Because Tammy had experienced this scenario many times throughout her career, she was quite used to charting unfamiliar territory. She rolled up her sleeves and went to work.[3]

There is always something to gain from our experiences, especially the painful ones.

WHAT *NOT* TO DO WHEN YOU'RE PASSED OVER

As Tammy and I both experienced, emotions surge when you're held back from taking the next step in your career. Being turned down feels personal. You've taken a risk, and it didn't turn out the way you hoped. You're left wondering how this rejection will affect the dynamics on your team or between you and your peers. How will it affect future advancement opportunities? All these questions create pressure, which can lead to poor choices about what you say and do as you face what happened.

Here are several actions *to avoid* when a promotion doesn't happen:

1. **React without hitting the pause button.** You'll be upset, disappointed, and even angry when you're first notified. Raw emotions place you at a higher risk of responding impulsively. You may say words or take actions you later regret, such as immediately resigning. To be transparent, when I was lying in bed recovering from surgery and nursing my emotional wounds, resigning was my first (and very emotional) thought!

2. **Pretend nothing happened.** If you're determined to act as if nothing happened, you'll miss out on the healing process. Denial also creates tension for other people, like those you lead and work closely with. You need to address the elephant in the room, so they don't feel as if they have to tiptoe around it. When my direct reports asked me if I was upset, I admitted I was. When they asked if I was quitting, I told them I was thinking through my next move, and they'd be the first to know.

3. **Compare yourself to others.** Comparing yourself to the person who received the promotion will either make you

feel inferior or superior; neither of these feelings will help you move toward God's best for you. In Tammy's case, she was aware of the gender bias she faced. She didn't focus on the people who got promoted; she focused on what she wanted to accomplish for the business.

4. **Blame yourself or other people.** Even if you only blame yourself, you're still starting a thought pattern that will trap you. Blame paralyzes you because it allows you to feel helpless. You're excused from taking responsibility, but you also can't move forward. If you get trapped here, it's easy to forget that change and growth are possible.

We may be tempted to take one or more of these actions because they're all rooted in emotion. When a negative situation happens, we naturally experience a range of feelings, but responding poorly detracts from the stewardship God has trusted us with and harms our integrity as leaders.

TIPS TO HELP YOU REGROUP AND RECOVER

The rest of the company found out about my missed opportunity before I did. No one sent a formal email, but gossip travels quickly. I'm grateful I didn't have to walk through the building and face questioning or sympathetic looks. I also didn't have to worry about facing the interview panel before I was ready. Not being in the office, however, didn't shield me from being asked tough questions by employees and peers:

How are you feeling about what happened?
What are you going to do?
Don't you feel cheated?

Everyone knew what had happened, and I felt humiliated. At the same time, the Holy Spirit helped me realize that humility was what I needed. I congratulated the other candidate with words, but my heart wasn't there yet. Whatever the reason behind it and whether a company is big or small, rejection takes up a lot of space. It almost seems impossible to step away from, but that's exactly the first step you need to take.

Process and manage your emotions. Set aside purposeful time to digest what happened and how you feel about it. Your confidence will be shaken, and you may start to doubt your abilities and accomplishments. Your feelings are important, so give yourself time and space to process them outside of work. Vent in your journal, and to your family, friends, and mentors—but set a limit for yourself. Talking through the missed promotion will allow you to gain a clearer perspective, but decide not to dwell there. Ask a friend or mentor to hold you accountable so you can turn the corner and start looking forward instead of backward.

Plan how you'll respond to tough questions. Be honest, authentic, but professional when people ask you how you feel. Here are some suggested responses:

> I'm disappointed, but I'm moving forward.
> I'm hurt, but I'm still committed to our team and the company.
> This experience has been hard, but I've also learned from it.

Gather feedback from others. Ask for feedback from the decision-maker(s), trusted peers, and mentors. Don't bring up the other candidate, but instead approach the conversation as an opportunity for self-improvement. Decide ahead of time not to argue or defend against what you hear. Humility leads to honesty, which helps you learn the truth and act on it. Feedback opens your eyes to how others see you; then you can decide if you want to change their perception or not.

In my quest for self-improvement, I asked a couple of colleagues for their feedback. They pointed out that I had missed specific political cues in my quest for career advancement. The last wave of people who held the position I was vying for all had the same career backgrounds; mine was the outlier. All the predecessors were men, a demographic I obviously didn't fit into. There were patterns of getting drinks after work or brainstorming on the ski slopes that I never took part in.

People close to me helped me see that, God's urging aside, I wasn't suited for the C-suite position. I didn't enjoy small talk or wining and dining people, and I preferred working with employees over external networking. Extensive travel would be required, and I was tired of traveling. My passions were developing high-performing people and teams and building robust systems. In short, I would have been miserable if they had promoted me.

This feedback wasn't easy to receive, but it affirmed that being rejected was a gift. Proverbs 27:17 was happening in real life as I listened to tough truths: "As iron sharpens iron, so one person sharpens another." Who from your life can you trust to (gently) sharpen you as you grow through your own painful rejection? Feedback itself is a gift, and it helps clarify the next best course of action.

Reflect on what you've learned. After processing what happened and gathering insights from others, begin to draw your own conclusions. The reflective process can reveal areas that stood between you and the new position. You might also use the process to explore why you wanted the promotion and if your "why" was misaligned. From experience, I suggest going through this exercise now, and a few months from now, because the immediate pain of being passed over will affect your perspective.

To start, identify your reasons for wanting to advance. Then think about why you didn't get promoted and brainstorm what you could do differently next time. Assess your fit for the position and explore your feelings again. Are you fired up and ready to prepare for the next promotion, or are you content to stay where you are and think about your next move? Do you feel relieved? Or have you decided to go in a completely new direction? Make time to reflect and record your thoughts, all the while remembering that your responses will change over time as you heal. Ask God to help you sift and sort through the situation. He'll show you what to pick up and what to lay down.

Plan and act. All the steps you've taken will help you understand what changes are needed in your professional development to achieve the role you want. The steps could also prompt you to reassess your career goals and the direction you're going. Like me, you may realize you were going in the wrong direction, and you need to change course. Whatever your realization, don't waste the gift of the experience: create a plan and follow it through.

There may be tangible steps to take, like being outspoken in meetings, taking the lead on high-profile projects, or networking more with peers. You may need to state your interest in future roles more assertively and clearly. Research and use external resources to help you strengthen certain skills, like communication or networking. If being passed over has pointed you toward a new career destination, set goals to get you there.

SACRED WORK

When we face modern workplace disappointments—like being passed over for a promotion that we hustled, hoped, and prayed for—we can also be tempted to think that God has rejected us too. But whether we invited God into every step or just the aftermath, He has been present the whole time, and His plans for us are still good. This situation caught you off guard, but God knew about it before it ever happened. His sovereignty and timeless plans are covering you right now. The process you went through had a purpose. God wants to reveal that purpose, and He will, just as He did with the many people in Scripture who felt passed over too.

While in prison, Joseph interprets the cupbearer's dream and asks the cupbearer to mention Joseph's plight to Pharaoh, so Pharaoh will release him. The cupbearer forgets about him, and Joseph is stuck in prison for two more years (see Gen. 40).

God closes Hannah's womb during a time when barren women were disgraced at best and divorced and abandoned at worst (see 1 Sam. 1).[4]

David is anointed the king of Israel and then reduced to hiding in caves and running for his life from Saul. He feels as if God has abandoned him (see 1 Sam. 21–30).

In each of these examples, the Bible also reveals the rest of the story. Pharaoh needs a couple of dreams interpreted, which prompts the cupbearer's memory. After revealing what Pharaoh's dreams mean, Joseph is appointed prime minister of Egypt, where God positions him to save his family from starvation and forgive the sins committed against him (see Gen. 41:12–41).

Hannah goes from being infertile and insulted to becoming known as a person whose faith and prayers produce Samuel, the anointer of King David and foreteller of Jesus (see 1 Sam. 1–2). Hannah's hope echoes forward through Samuel's words, announcing the coming of our once and future King, the Messiah (see 1 Sam. 2:7 and Acts 3:24).

After fifteen years of running and hiding, David is anointed the King of Judah. An important descendant comes from David's line, one whose kingdom and reign will last forever, our very own Jesus (see Pss. 110 and 132).

God was at work behind the scenes to enact the best plans for those who felt skipped, overlooked, and forgotten. Even so, outcomes may not match what we envisioned or hoped for. God may be telling you no or He may be telling you not yet, but He is always weaving our story to point others to Jesus. Whatever the outcome, know that God sees you and is with you. Be willing to trust that even when you feel like someone has intentionally tried to harm you, He will use it for good. Forgive them, fix your eyes on Jesus, and live confidently knowing that even if you can't see the complete picture yet, His plans for you are always good.

When You Need to Address Performance

Procrastination usually results in sorrowful regret.
Today's duties put off until tomorrow give us a double burden to bear;
the best way is to do them in their proper time.[1]

IDA SCOTT TAYLOR MCKINNEY, AUTHOR AND AMERICAN SONGWRITER

No matter what the issues are, addressing performance within your own team is never easy. Your employees may be talented and competent but miss deadlines or lack interpersonal skills. Sometimes your team members may have a difficult time working together, and other times they've simply become complacent and need a gentle push to keep improving. When a leader hires someone, she hopes the new employee's skills are a solid match for the results that are needed. Yet sometimes there's a gap that requires intentional coaching.

If you're consistently observing an employee's performance and providing feedback, it's easy to deal with specific problems as they come up. However, if you wait until the struggles are impossible to ignore to assess and address them, you've done a disservice to your employee and you've made your job more difficult. When we ignore an employee's shortcomings, the consequences spread to every corner of our organization.

HOW CAN WE SUPPORT POSITIVE CHANGE IN OUR EMPLOYEES?

Effective, caring stewardship is active and requires you to correct and coach employees as soon as a problem surfaces. When you actively manage performance, you help your team make effective changes so they can improve and reach their full potential. I learned the value of this principle long before I became a leader.

When I was a teen, I fell in love with running. Competing in high school track and cross-country helped me pay for college and led to my first teaching job. I credit all of this to my high school coach. The first day of track practice, Coach Kimsey had us run warm-up laps and then intervals. After practice, he called me away from the team and said, "You're fast, but you can be even faster. At practice tomorrow, I want you to run with these." He handed me two aluminum batons, the kind used in a relay. I just stared at him. I was a freshman from a broken home living with my fifth family in two years, and I already felt like an oddball. Now he wanted me to practice while carrying batons?! "You cross your arms when you run," he said. "You've probably done it your whole life. It's inefficient, affects your gait, and slows you down. The batons force you to run without crossing your arms."

I shook my head no.

He put one hand on my shoulder. "Look, it's simple. I think you have a future in running, and it can take you far, but it's up to you. Deal with the batons for a few weeks or stay mediocre."

I ran with those batons for a month. I got faster, won more races, and never forgot that lesson. Years later, when I needed to motivate employees to improve their performance, I followed the same principles Coach Kimsey used with me:

Correct employees privately.

Address problems as soon as you see them.

Stick to one issue.

Be clear about what needs to change.

Explain how the change benefits the employee.

Focus on the bigger picture.

Emphasize that the employee owns the decision to change and improve.

I've found this approach effective when addressing most performance issues—regardless of their nature or root cause. Employees will intuitively know if you have their best interest at heart, and that determines how they respond to your advice. Coaching employees requires courage, intention, and investment, but it's an effective way to help them get back on track. Even in the most stressful situations, your desire to do what's best for the employee and the organization will help ensure success.

IS PART OF THE EMPLOYEE'S
PERFORMANCE ISSUE YOUR FAULT?

Like every member of your team, you have room for improvement too. Any time an employee's performance falls short, humbly examine how you may have contributed to the problem. You'll want a clear grasp on what part is your responsibility before you address the issue with your employee.

Ask these questions to help you determine your role in someone else's performance issue:

> *Has this type of performance issue happened before with other employees?* For example, if several new hires have struggled to perform their jobs, maybe there's a problem with the onboarding process or the training program, or perhaps expectations are unclear. Have other employees in your department failed to meet goals because of workload? This could point to your need to change how you distribute workload.

> *Have you taken the time to develop a trusting relationship with your employee?* Employees want to do their jobs well, and they don't want to disappoint their leaders or departments. They may struggle to speak up about obstacles that interfere with their ability to succeed because they don't want to lose your favor. The stronger the trust between you and your employees, the more likely they are to tell you about what's hindering their success—before it affects performance.

> *Do you regularly provide positive and negative feedback?* Discussions about performance need to be part of the regular conversations you have with your team. These conversations should include constructive criticism, clear expectations, and praise for work well done. If feedback only happens when troubles arise, you're failing to give your employees the communication they need to succeed.

After you've thought about your possible role in an employee's performance problem, it's time to dig into the root cause. All people are nuanced, which makes it hard to find what's really behind a performance issue. While an issue may appear straightforward, you'll find that the reasons behind it tend to be complicated and multidimensional.

MEETING ONE: FIND THE ROOT CAUSE

The difference between how the employee is performing now and where they need to be is called a performance gap, and there is always a reason for this disparity. Until you and the employee agree on the root cause(s), you can't identify ways to solve them. First, you'll prepare for an initial meeting with your employee where you'll discuss performance concerns. Then you'll get back together in a second meeting to address solutions. Here are six steps you can take to prepare for and hold an effective first meeting where you'll determine what is causing an employee to struggle.

1. **Look for exceptions and patterns.** If an employee rarely misses a deadline, then one missed deadline isn't a pattern, it's an exception. If an employee has had this difficulty since being hired, that's a pattern. Exceptions and patterns each tell different stories and require different actions.

2. **Review your recent communication.** Before addressing a problem with your employee, review recent meetings and conversations, so your perspective is more accurate. When was your last conversation? Have you consistently made time to engage with them? Has the employee shared anything about workload, personal problems, or job-related stress? If the issue has been ongoing, were you clear in addressing your concerns? Did the employee understand your expectations?

   During this step, you may discover or be reminded of important insights from previous discussions. You may even discover you were supposed to follow through with an action the employee needed you to take, but you overlooked it.

3. **Prepare for the conversation.** A productive conversation requires thought and planning. Before you meet, jot down your ideas, insights, and questions, and then prepare for the meeting by creating an outline. The goal of the conversation is to identify the root cause and help your employee move forward.

4. **Have the conversation and frame it for success.** The more at ease employees are, the more freely they can communicate. Check in on a personal note to put the employee at ease and set a positive tone. Then ask questions, without accusing.

   Use your notes or outline to guide you through your conversation with your employee but be open to what you can learn from them too. Expect that new information may change the conclusion or ideas you'd prepared ahead of time and be flexible. What you knew a few weeks ago may be different now.

5. **Be present and listen!** Be open to receive what your employee has to say and give them your full attention. Listen for nuances in their stories, such as how they feel or what they've been thinking about, while they explain their perspective.

6. **Clarify the root cause(s).** The root cause they name may not match the conclusions you made as you prepared for the meeting, but this step is collaborative and the key to resolution. After listening, if you still disagree with their perspective, say so, but commit to giving it more thought. Don't get caught up in debating or defending. You'll both have time to process the conversation before taking the next steps. Paraphrase the employee's perspective back to them to make sure there aren't any misunderstandings. Document both

of your perspectives, and send your notes to the employee afterward, so you're on the same page.

You've identified the root cause. What's next? It's a good idea to end the first meeting by agreeing to regroup within a few days (or a week at most). A brief delay gives you both a chance to digest what you talked about and individually brainstorm ways to address the performance issue. The second meeting is when you'll both come prepared with solutions.

Be clear with your employee about how to prepare for the next meeting and what you expect them to bring. For example, "I want to be a resource and help you do your best work. What are some ways I could help you improve? Let me know what you come up with." If your root causes are different, you could say something like, "I understand your perspective, and I'll think more about what you said. I'd also like you to consider my idea and bring suggestions for resolution to the next meeting."

Here's an example from my career: I hired an inventory analyst who made errors in reporting for weeks after her training. We launched a retraining, but the errors continued. Other departments relied on her reports and analysis to do their jobs, so the impact was significant. When I discussed the problem with her, she felt her training wasn't adequate. The person who trained her was detail-oriented and an excellent trainer, so I was doubtful. I'd noticed that the analyst regularly finished her work early and asked around for other tasks, so my perspective was she rushed through her work. I thought maybe she was skipping steps, so I talked to the trainer. He said the analyst didn't ask questions and was quick to voice her understanding.

In my first performance meeting with the analyst, I acknowledged our different perspectives: I thought she was rushing through her work and perhaps underestimating its importance. What I heard from her was that her training was inadequate. Then, I asked her to think about ways to solve her suggested root cause and mine. More to come on this story shortly!

When the root cause is personal. If the root cause is personal, the follow-up meeting requires different preparation and takes on a different tone. Think about how frequently personal challenges have affected the employee's ability to do their job and what assistance you can offer within company policy. Depending on the circumstance, you may feel an exception to policy is warranted, so be prepared to advocate for one. Work with your company to outline tangible ways you can support the employee, based on the individual challenge and their specific needs.

For example, an employee may have unexpected demands because of caregiving, health issues, or changes in childcare. You can work with human resources to explore flexible schedule options. Stressful life events may indicate that your employee needs professional assistance or to take vacation, unpaid leave, or job-protected leave. Employees who are under personal strain often shy away from asking for help in their professional lives. They try to compartmentalize personal away from professional, and a conversation about performance may be the first time they open up. Once they do, you have an opportunity and obligation to support them.

Set the next meeting. After you've identified the root cause(s), promptly schedule your second meeting. You want to take advantage of the momentum from your first meeting and show that quickly implementing solutions is important. Make sure your employee knows to come to the second meeting prepared with solutions.

Create a Plan

In addressing root causes, employees need to do the heavy lifting, but leaders still need to take part in creating a corrective plan. You can't view this issue as solely the employee's. Your responsibility is to provide guidance and direction as you work on the plan together. Due diligence on your part includes outlining a comprehensive plan for resolution, so your employee can follow your suggestions and be successful.

Examples of actions you may need to take:

- If expectations weren't clear or have created workload issues, clarify and change expected outcomes and priorities. A survey by ClearCompany found that "only around 50% of employees would 'strongly agree' they know what's expected of them at work."[2] Imagine how much better people and companies would perform if expectations were clear!
- If there are workplace obstacles, create a plan to remove them. You may need to increase system access, provide additional training and resources, or confront people who are interfering with your employee's ability to perform.
- If you've neglected to meet consistently with and support a new hire, restructure your schedule to incorporate regular check-ins. Resolve to be more observant and engaged.

MEETING TWO: TALK ABOUT AND IMPLEMENT SOLUTIONS

The goal of the second meeting is to agree on solutions and how to implement them. Here are suggestions for a successful regroup:

1. Begin by summarizing the performance gap that occurred and explain that the goal of this meeting is to tackle the root cause.
2. Let the employee know you have ideas to discuss but invite them to share their ideas first.

3. Listen attentively, take notes, and ask questions. If your employee seems hesitant or apprehensive, gently encourage them to be honest. Repeat suggestions back to make sure you understood them correctly.

4. When it's your turn to share ideas, keep the discussion focused on making improvements for the future instead of rehashing details from the first meeting. Be transparent and sincere about how you may have contributed to the issue and the changes you intend to make.

5. Conclude by bulleting the actions you'll take moving forward and have your employee do the same. Email them a copy of your notes for future reference.

Here's how this looked in my story about the inventory analyst: When we met, she suggested having the trainer watch her run the reports and write her analysis from start to finish. She had demonstrated parts of it before, but never completed the whole task while supervised. I thought this was a great idea and told her so. Next, I offered my suggestion. I wanted her to better understand how her job impacted others, so I asked her to sit with other departments so she could see firsthand how they relied on her work to complete theirs. She wasn't excited about this, but when we talked about its significance, she was on board.

Next, I asked the trainer to join us. He liked the analyst's suggestion but requested that she also explain her process to him as she did it. This would help him pinpoint areas where the analyst was going through the motions but didn't grasp what all the steps meant. The analyst was resistant to this, but I reminded her that we wanted her to succeed. We weren't trying to trip her up; we were trying to come alongside her and help her move forward. The trainer also emphasized the importance of asking questions, not just during the training, but at any point afterward. He explained that taking longer was better than rushing and delivering a faulty analysis.

In the end, the trainer was able to troubleshoot problem areas, and the analyst finally became comfortable asking questions. The trainer invested patience and encouragement, and that investment paid off. After seeing how much time the sales and accounting departments lost because of her errors, the analyst better understood how critical her accuracy was. Though bumpy at first, the road eventually led to a happy ending.

Support the plan. It's important to encourage your employee routinely so they stay engaged in the improvement process without becoming overwhelmed by it. Proactively provide and ask for updates during your regular one-on-ones. These regular check-ins on employee performance and progress should be a natural part of your communication already. Compliment employees as they make improvements and give them constructive feedback when needed. Once you think the situation has stabilized, ask how they're feeling about their progress. If they're in agreement, move the issue to the back burner.

Act quickly if the performance issue resurfaces. When you work hard for a resolution, it can be painful and disappointing if an issue resurfaces. But when it does, you have to act quickly and not ignore it. If you implemented solutions but the performance gap isn't closing, take the next step according to company policy. Because you've communicated openly and regularly with the employee, they shouldn't be surprised when you take further action.

Concluding thoughts: I know this coaching process is intense, but I also know you are up for it! You believe in your employee, you want what's best for them, and you're committed to help them achieve their potential. God has given you leadership savvy, emotional intelligence, and a godly heart. You are more than equipped.

SACRED WORK

My child, don't reject the LORD's discipline, and don't be upset when he corrects you. For the LORD corrects those he loves, just as a father corrects a child in whom he delights. Joyful is the person who finds wisdom, the one who gains understanding.

PROVERBS 3:11–13 NLT

When we think about managing performance, we may feel uneasy or unprepared. I never received training on how to give constructive feedback or correct employee performance, and most leaders I've met are in the same boat. Expressing gratitude and extending compliments feels natural and positive, but assessing and confronting performance gaps can feel negative and harsh. Even if we're comfortable with confrontation, coaching employees to help them maximize their skills and potential looks a little different. One helpful example we can look to is how and why God corrects us.

As our Father, mentor, and ultimate leader, God is constantly affirming and correcting us. Throughout Scripture, we read about the depth of His love, patience, and kindness. The Bible also explains that because of God's love, He doesn't hesitate to discipline us or let us experience consequences. This is how He teaches us, renews us, and brings us into a closer relationship with Him. As we grow in our faith, we are both affirmed and corrected; this rhythm carries us forward. The lessons we learn from being loved and taught will bring us joy and equip us for our next steps.

In a similar way, we're entrusted to affirm and correct our employees. We have the honor and responsibility of loving them well and helping them become the best version of themselves. When we build relationships with the intention of loving and stewarding, the fear and dread that can hover around performance issues goes away.

Pray for your employees and the best outcome for them. You may see a complete turnaround in performance, or the employee may decide this job isn't the right fit for them and decide to leave. I've had former employees circle back to me and say that getting fired or receiving correction was a gift because of what they learned or a new career path they took. If we coach wisely and wholeheartedly, employees will benefit whether they stay or go.

I've been where you are, and I understand how difficult it is to feel responsible for another person. Remember: you can influence an employee's performance, but you can't control the outcome. As I wrote this chapter, I prayed that God would give you:

discernment to see beyond what's apparent,

wisdom to know what to say and when,

clarity to build the most effective coaching strategy,

patience to invest time and heart into the process, and

courage to let go after.

Take heart! God goes before you. He will establish your plans and work through you to accomplish good things (see Prov. 16:3 and Jer. 29:11).

15

How to Build a Culture That Attracts and Retains Talent

It's too easy to blame human resources when the work culture is weak. Leaders affect the work environment every day. They're the ones who need to spot weaknesses in the culture. They're the ones who need to understand what the organization has to gain and what it has to lose.[1]

NANCY J. LEWIS, DEI EXPERT AND CEO OF PROGRESSIVE TECHNIQUES, INC.

Whether a business is steady or slow, finding and keeping a talented workforce can be a challenge. A company needs to manage talent well, and that responsibility reaches far beyond the human resources department. Depending on the size of the company and its organizational structure, a leader's involvement in the recruiting and hiring process will vary. But every leader has the ability to affect workplace culture, which in turn influences hiring and retention. Leaders need to spearhead initiatives that foster remarkable workplace cultures, which will attract and keep remarkable people.

WHAT IS WORKPLACE CULTURE,
AND WHY IS IT IMPORTANT?

Forbes summarizes work culture as the collective attitudes, behaviors, and beliefs of an organization.[2] Culture creates a company's personality and affects how people feel when they're at work and how they feel about each other. It shapes how employees view their jobs and how committed they are to their companies. I'm sure your work culture is an important part of what keeps you happy and motivated too.

When I was the vice president at Petzl America, visitors were often surprised to see a climbing wall next to our warehouse. Petzl manufactures equipment for work and recreation in vertical spaces (picture firefighters and rock climbers), but visitors inevitably said, "What about the liability?" and "Insurance must cost a fortune!"

We had it covered. We invested time and money upfront in research, attorney fees, and putting protocols into place. As an outdoor company full of active people who were passionate about vertical access, everyone agreed it was worth the investment. Planning, building, and maintaining the wall became a community effort, with most employees pitching in. These efforts reflected another company value: creating community. A strong culture is one where individuals understand the culture, believe in it, and feel connected to it.

In the ever-changing, uncertain world of work, workplace culture remains the anchor and heart for companies of all sizes.[3] PricewaterhouseCoopers conducted a survey of 3,200 workers from various companies, and 67 percent of respondents said that culture is more important than strategy or operations.[4] Leaders I polled across ten industries on LinkedIn summarized the following advantages of having a stable, established culture:

- Topnotch new hires
- High engagement
- Employee longevity
- Better customer experiences
- More successful change initiatives[5]

Other studies echo these advantages, along with higher returns on investment and stronger market resilience.[6] Leaders who value a strong culture value their employees. The challenge comes in building these cultures one pillar at a time and ensuring that what leaders believe about company culture matches up with what workers experience.

SIX ACTIONS THAT STRENGTHEN COMPANY CULTURE

In 2023, O.C. Tanner Institute's culture report showed that purpose, belonging, growth, and balance are what people want from their companies.[7] These findings provide leaders with opportunities because prioritizing these values doesn't require a huge budget or unlimited resources. You can survey workers to assess the cultural landscape within your specific organization, but there are a few big hitters at the forefront regardless of industry and company size.[8] I've taken those big hitters and translated them into actions you can take to strengthen your workplace culture:

1. Practice flexibility as a reflection of balance. Flexible schedules are difficult to wrangle because preferences may look different for each person on your team. You may have a lot of autonomy to allow varying types of flexibility, or you may only have a little. Either way, communicate openly about what you can and can't do and then ask your team to identify and rank their flexibility requests. Some may need to work from home more than others. Some may need to start and end their days earlier than everyone else. Take the guesswork out and ask them.

Many companies allow leaders to work around core business hours. For example, if company policy requires workers to be present or available from 9:00 a.m. to 2:00 p.m., you still have a sizable chunk of the week where you can allow flexible schedules. If this isn't a company policy, lobby to make it one. You're not the only leader who wants to support your team by helping them with work-life balance. Build alliances and push for change.

2. Prioritize employee well-being. Since the pandemic was declared in 2020, work and life outside of work have blended together. Professional and personal lives exist inside the same compartment, most times literally, and the formerly hard lines between personal and professional have blurred. This shift opens the door for you to express interest and concern about how your team is faring without overstepping boundaries. If you notice someone is showing signs of stress, talk to the person privately. "You're more quiet than usual. Is everything okay?" The person may share stress about a personal or work issue. If the issue is personal, listen and acknowledge what they're saying. Be empathetic and make sure they know about available resources, such as taking a personal day or access to employee assistance programs.

If a work issue is straining the individual's personal life, offer solutions. Maybe they have too many competing priorities. You can clarify priorities, remove some, or put one or two on the back burner. If your employee has experienced a change in their family life, they may need a new schedule or some time off. Offer reassurances and collaborate on a resolution.

3. Foster community. Simple rhythms like team, department, and all-hands meetings build stability and give teams something to count on. In the same way that established traditions help us feel connected to our families, routine gatherings can nurture a sense of belonging in the workplace. Intentionally structure meetings as a space where teams can ask questions, share concerns, and celebrate milestones. This becomes one way that individuals are knitted together, whether the work environment is on-site, virtual, or hybrid.

> **Provide creative opportunities for your team members to engage with you and each other.**

To further build community, provide creative opportunities for your team members to engage with you and each other. Be innovative and develop activities that will be enjoyable for everyone. Old standbys like open video hangouts will feel like forced fun and won't produce great team-bonding results. Here are a few suggestions:

- Empower teams to suggest and implement traditions.
- Organize a service meetup where your team volunteers together.
- Routinely acknowledge accomplishments and express gratitude.
- Create programs where employees can thank and recognize one another.

4. Be proactive with professional development. Don't wait for your direct reports to approach you about career advancement. Integrate this topic into your one-to-ones early and often. Ask questions like: If you could do anything at this company, what would it be? Where do you see yourself in a year, three years, five years? What's one skill you'd like to develop? What's your idea of success?

When you discover what their goals, ambitions, and dreams are, you become equipped to advocate on their behalf. If an individual wants to move into a leadership role but isn't sure how to do that now, provide low-risk opportunities. Have them lead minor projects or a volunteer outing. Be intentional in mentoring them in leadership-related areas and have them spend time with other leaders. Professional development also includes learning new skills, working with other departments, and being empowered to solve team problems.

5. Communicate purpose and instill it. When people can link their work to a broader purpose, they stop focusing on "me" and start focusing on "we." Individuals want to do meaningful work; they want jobs that have a purpose and make a difference.

My husband worked for a medical device company where managers and leaders had access to a growing library of video stories featuring people whose lives were saved because of the technology and innovation of the company. Workers saw firsthand the difference they made and why quality, protocols, and costs were important. Watching these videos connected people to the broader purpose of saving lives and improving the health of consumers. This connection energized everyone: leaders, managers, quality control technicians, and frontline teams. They all understood the "why" behind their everyday jobs.

In some companies, purpose may not be tied to a worker's job, but it can still be a powerful catalyst for engagement. At Petzl, for instance, sustainability was a valued part of the work culture. We recycled before it was popular, offered discounted bus passes, and encouraged people to store their bikes at their desks if they wanted to commute to work. Employees enjoyed being part of a company that was purposeful in how it treated the environment.

6. Be a trustworthy, authentic leader. Software provider Good-Hire conducted a survey of 3,000 full-time workers across ten industries. An astounding 82 percent say they would quit their jobs because of a poor manager or leader.[9] Your relationship with your direct reports directly affects their job satisfaction, and trust has to be at the heart of that relationship. Employees don't want transactional relationships where they feel important only as far as they benefit you or the company. One way to foster trust is to follow through on commitments. Be consistent and timely with performance reviews, pay increases, and changes or exceptions to policy.

Another important leadership behavior is authenticity, which includes being vulnerable and making room for others to do the same. A friend who leads an engineering group disclosed to her team the stress she felt trying to meet everyone's different needs for flexible scheduling. Another shared with her direct reports how frustrating it was to build team traditions because of their obvious cynicism. In both cases, these leaders led with transparency and what followed were candid conversations that translated into solutions. Your willingness to be vulnerable and open will compel your direct reports to do the same.

CULTURAL COMPLEXITIES WE CAN'T GIVE UP ON

Diversity, equity, and inclusion should matter to us because they are the outworking of a critical truth embedded deeply within the Christian faith. The truth is that despite our differences, we were all made equally in God's image and ultimately belong to God and to each other.[10]

DR. ARTHUR L. SATTERWHITE III, VICE PRESIDENT OF DIVERSITY, BELONGING, AND STRATEGY AT YOUNG LIFE

I was on the *Biblical Leadership @ Work* podcast and the host, Jason Woodward, asked, "What do you think the biggest gap in leadership is right now in the faith community?" My answer was that I'd love leaders to advocate for individuals who aren't in their own demographic. For example, white professionals need to care about the challenges people of color experience in the workplace. Men need to help with obstacles women are facing. Boomers and Gen Xers need to understand what's important to millennials and Gen Zers. And—vice versa for all. We need to stop seeing our workplace from inside silos and instead reach through the silos and help each other.

I hope that as Christian leaders, we won't be satisfied with easy wins, but instead we'd run after workplace issues that are gritty and bruising even. This is the space where the values of diversity, equity, and inclusion (DEI) exist. Companies with DEI programs want to support individuals who may otherwise be marginalized, such as women, veterans, and people of different ethnicities, physical abilities, ages, and religions.

My friend Nancy Lewis is an expert on the topic. Her company, Progressive Techniques, Inc., coaches businesses and executives to "develop their people potential."[11] Since Nancy and her company provide DEI consulting services, I asked her perspective on the topic and how it can strengthen or weaken workplace culture. These are key takeaways from our conversation:

Diversity initiatives without measurable outcomes do more harm than good. Diversity initiatives are policies and practices created to make workplace experiences better for groups like women and people of color. The popularity of these initiatives ebbs and flows with societal events and public awareness. If companies simply want to check a box, they create marketing blurbs, but this doesn't create accountability, which is the only way initiatives become part of the culture. Nancy calls this "window dressing," and the new workforce (millennials and Gen Zers) won't tolerate it.[12] Millennials, in particular, are a generation extremely capable of researching beyond marketing fluff. They're also unafraid to hop jobs until they find a company whose values align with theirs.

Nancy explains millennials (generally defined as those born between 1981 and 1996) want to work for companies and leaders who care about improving the world. They want to work for leaders they can trust, and they want strong diversity policies. Aside from wanting to create an equitable workplace, why should leaders pay attention to what this generation thinks? According to the U.S. Bureau of Labor Statistics, millennials make up 35 percent of the workforce.[13] They are the largest generation of workers.

To breathe life into diversity initiatives, leaders can model what they want the company to reflect. They have to be invested in change and committed to defined and tracked outcomes. As Nancy says, "Culture starts small and builds."[14] Leaders can start by using metrics and creating a plan based on questions like these: What are our current demographics? What are the flaws with our current initiative? What do we want to see instead? By when? What steps will take us there? What complications exist and how can we overcome them? How will we hold ourselves accountable?

Equity and equality mean significantly different things. Equity means each individual gets the resources, opportunities, or support they need to reach an equal outcome.

Nancy uses a visual to explain the differences. She says imagine three people standing behind a 7-foot fence, trying to watch a sporting event. One is 4'6", another 5'6", and the last is 6'. None of them can see over the fence, so equality gives each of them a 1-foot box to stand on. Two of them still can't see over the fence. To solve the problem, equity gives each person the number of boxes they need to have an equal vantage. Creating an equitable environment means leaders remove barriers individuals face because of how they're different.

For example, if a company requires every warehouse technician to work overtime on the weekend, that's equality. Every person is treated the same. But if one technician needs to be off on Sundays for religious reasons and can make up the hours on other days, that's equity.

Microaggressions are the enemy of equity and inclusivity. I asked Nancy what she sees as the most toxic leadership behavior threatening healthy work cultures today. She said, "Leaders who initiate or allow microaggressions create toxic pockets in the workplace that damage the culture." Microaggressions are actions resulting from unconscious bias. Everyone has this bias, which means we make assumptions or judgments about people without even realizing it. These types of assumptions form based on how we grew up, how we're conditioned by society, and how our brain handles information.

> DEI is an area where leaders can make a significant difference, and Christian leaders need to be at the forefront.

When microaggressions surface, they show up as comments, snubs, or nonverbal actions that negatively affect the individuals they're directed toward. For example, Nancy says assertive professional Black women are frequently accused of being aggressive or bossy. More subtle microaggressions include not recruiting women, older candidates, or people of color, or failing to support their professional advancement. In order to address unconscious bias and behaviors like these that can result from it, leaders can:

Be aware of their own biased tendencies.

Immediately address microaggressions they witness.

Create a confidential reporting process for others.

Provide training about unconscious bias and micro-aggressions.

Conclusion: This issue is complex because companies may try to force DEI policies into practice without thoughtfully considering all the factors. For example, they might require a certain percentage of women candidates or people of color without putting the work into standardizing hiring practices or finding qualified candidates. Programs can also unintentionally create division, with employees becoming focused on ethnicity, gender, and age. There is nothing easy about this topic, but DEI is an area where leaders can make a significant difference, and Christian leaders need to be at the forefront. DEI work is grueling, dear leader, but the most arduous work is often what's most needed.

WHAT DO YOUR EMPLOYEES THINK?

A timeless tension exists between how leaders view work culture and how employees experience it. This gap is where your efforts to strengthen the culture need to begin, and your first step is to provide time and space for workers to share their viewpoints. There is no substitute for honest feedback from the teams you steward; they are the people you're responsible for, and how they experience corporate culture is what ultimately matters.

SACRED WORK

I love the example of hiring, retention, and diversity that we see with Jesus and His disciples. In *The Gospel on the Ground* Bible study, Kristi McLelland explains how Jesus chooses and gathers His team. Jesus was a student before He became a teacher. Only one out of a thousand students became teachers, or rabbis, as Jesus did.[15] Students flocked to rabbis, asking to be accepted as followers. Jesus didn't indulge in this practice. Instead, He went out and chose His followers.[16] From the minute they were on His team, the followers of Jesus knew they were valued. His onboarding process spoke volumes to His people from the very beginning.

This team was made up of men from different backgrounds, of different occupations, and with distinct personalities (see Matt. 4:18–22; 9:9; Mark 3:13–19). Jesus didn't choose disciples who were like Him; He chose men who saw His leadership and then became like Him. Jesus kept the disciples close and modeled leadership through every encounter, always showing mercy, kindness, truth, and strength. He took care of their spiritual and physical needs, and they saw Him do the same for others. Instruction, correction, and accountability were at the center of their relationship, but so were love, compassion, and empowerment. This mighty legacy pushed the gospel outward, brought God's kingdom down to earth, and spread it to the corners of the ancient world (see Acts 1:8).

As a follower of Jesus, you have the ability to show up like Him and lead like Him. What a wonder to think that the Son of God was also a leader of people. He knew what it was like to assemble a team. Jesus understood what people needed and how to provide for them. He led by example, so we would have the best example to follow. Because you know Him, you can lead like Him. There's no better work culture you can build than one that reflects the kingdom of God.

16

The Power of
Mentorship

If you cannot see where you are going,
ask someone who has been there before.[1]

J LOREN NORRIS, LEADERSHIP AND STRATEGIC COMMUNICATION COACH

Mentorship is vital for leaders. It's why I founded the Sacred
Work ministry, where I provide free career and leadership
coaching for women, and it's why I wanted to author this book. When
women say *yes* to leadership, they also say *yes* to high-risk decisions,
unwieldy problems, and a range of professional challenges. Because
of the many stressors leaders face, strengthening women as leaders
has incredible value. I like to use the hard experiences and failures
I've faced to mentor other women leaders, because one positive outcome of learning the hard way is helping others learn the easy way.
I call this *recycled strength*, a term inspired by 2 Corinthians 1:3–4:

> Praise be to the God and Father of our Lord Jesus Christ, the
> Father of compassion and the God of all comfort, who com-
> forts us in all our troubles, so that we can comfort those in
> any trouble with the comfort we ourselves receive from God.

Recycled strength happens when God comforts and strengthens Christian leaders through challenges, and they become equipped to strengthen others facing the same struggles. What a legacy of faith and one that's especially important for women as they embrace their work as valued and seen by God. Sometimes we need to feel valued and seen by another person—someone who has fought doubt and discouragement and who has felt conflicted, unseen, and unimportant. Because God made a way for us, we can repurpose our faith and make a way for others.

When I started mentoring women, I was too naïve to overthink the process, and that was a gift. Have you ever made a commitment and later reflected, "If I'd known how difficult this would be, I may not have done it!" God is good to invite us quietly into big adventures in understated ways. The Holy Spirit often moves us to say "yes" before we even realize He's asked the question.

I've talked to women leaders who either want to find a mentor or become one. Both groups are hesitant or overwhelmed about taking the first step. Potential mentors talk themselves out of mentorship because they assume they're not qualified. Their hearts are open and ready, but they've convinced themselves they have nothing to offer. Imposter syndrome sneaks around and steals just enough confidence to keep them still. Women who want a mentor aren't sure how to approach someone. They're afraid of rejection, and they pile up a stack of "what ifs." Do either of these scenarios describe you? If so, you're in the right place.

I've collaborated with two remarkable women, and with our combined experiences, we'll help you become a mentor or find one. Catherine Gates served as the executive director of Women in the Marketplace (WiM),[2] a nonprofit whose mission is to equip working women to pursue their faith and careers confidently for God's glory. Before leading WiM, Catherine was a corporate leader in the technology industry. Erica Dvorak is a marketing expert who worked for startups and Fortune 500 companies before pivoting into a new career. She's now the founder of Faith & Gather, a lifestyle media brand for Christian women, and she hosts the *Faith Inspired Podcast*. Catherine, Erica, and I have all been mentors and benefited from having mentors ourselves. I'll share our collective observations and knowledge so you can replace your hesitation with confidence and enthusiasm.

WHAT IS A MENTOR?

Walk with the wise and become wise.

PROVERBS 13:20

We sometimes overcomplicate what it means to mentor someone, but Merriam-Webster offers a simple, clarifying definition for *mentor*: "a trusted counselor or guide."[3] The Collins English Dictionary defines *mentor* as "a wise, loyal advisor; a teacher or coach."[4] These simple definitions are liberating because they shatter any preconceived ideas about mentorship, which can be convoluted and hard to pin down. Now we begin to see how we can mentor the people we lead at work, those inside our companies or industries, and people we meet at church or in our communities. We can also find mentors in these same places; the opportunities are endless.

HOW DO YOU KNOW IF YOU'RE READY TO BE A MENTOR?

Each of us has something to offer someone else. We may have knowledge, experience, or the ability to listen and encourage. Our stories and career journeys equip us to give back to others what someone gave to us—or many times, what we wished for but didn't have. Perhaps you realize this, and you're compelled to be more intentional in pouring into others. As Christians, this may come as the Holy Spirit nudging you. You pause because you recognize the value of mentoring, but the commitment is scary, and you wonder if you have anything to offer.

Mentorship can be small and simple or big and structured.

Catherine explains this tension well: "There are a couple of fear-based barriers standing between women and mentorship. One is self-doubt. Women question their abilities and if they're capable of helping others. The other barrier is the time commitment. Women leaders are overworked, juggling a host of responsibilities, and time-starved. They're afraid to commit because they already don't have enough time in their lives. What if they can't follow through?"[5]

There are other barriers too. You may conclude you're not ready because you need to learn more or gain more experience before you're an expert. Or you may dwell on flaws or habits you need to overcome before you're qualified. These obstacles block you from what you understand God is calling you to do. Remember: fear and striving are not welcome visitors in your life! If God is urging you to counsel, guide, or coach other women, you're ready.

Mentorship can be small and simple or big and structured. How you approach coming alongside others may begin small and grow into something big. Obedience doesn't require extravagance; it requires willingness. Your yes simply means you agree with His calling and trust Him to show you what's next. God gives us intelligence, discernment, and the power of choice. Inside your obedience, you'll find tremendous freedom and agency.

Mentoring may look like having a monthly one-hour lunch with an aspiring leader, volunteering for a formal mentorship program, or something in between. Maybe your story shows someone she's not alone as she faces workplace inequity. Maybe your experience helps prevent a new leader from making the same mistake you did. Or perhaps your listening ear and trusted advice assist a new Christian when work situations challenge her integrity. If the Holy Spirit prompts you, He already has something specific in mind.

MENTORING YOUR TEAM

Not all leaders are mentors, and not all mentors are leaders. Leadership and career experts debate questions such as, "Should leaders function as mentors?" and "Are employees better served by mentors who are not their bosses?"[6] Those who think leaders should not be mentors believe a leader's primary responsibilities are motivating, steering, and pushing departments for outcomes and results.[7] Companies who agree with this view have formal programs matching mentors to employees who don't report to them. Their reasoning is that employees can develop a closer relationship and share more openly with someone who isn't their boss.[8] For these same reasons, some employees only seek mentors outside their organizations.

On the flip side, other experts argue that the best leaders are mentors too.[9] Based on my experience and conversations with other professionals, employees whose bosses can be both leaders and mentors stand to benefit significantly.

When Erica worked for a Fortune 500 company, her director was more transactional than relational. She was a powerful leader, but not a mentor. When the director left, she was replaced by Thomas, who understood the value of combining mentorship with leadership. He asked Erica about her aspirations, what she loved about her work, and what professional or personal support she needed. Erica explained that while everyone on her team worked sixty-plus hours a week, she was the only parent. Other team members couldn't relate to her situation. So Thomas connected her with a peer mentor who was also a mom to young children. The mentor and Erica met monthly to talk about the struggles of balancing a career with motherhood and how to handle those challenges. By making this connection for Erica, Thomas showed a vested interest in her overall wellbeing.

Erica and her team worked long hours in a high-stress environment, but because Thomas worked side-by-side with them, they remained motivated. He maintained a high level of awareness because he experienced what they experienced. Despite a hectic, packed work week, he faithfully kept his one-on-one meetings with each team member. He created a strong team environment that centered on the care he took with individuals.

I've heard other examples, similar to Erica's, that applaud leaders who can both lead and mentor. Here are three helpful tips to become this kind of leader:

1. **Pay attention to the complete well-being of your employees.** In Erica's case, Thomas understood that what went on outside her work life was important to her and affected how she viewed her work. Because he asked specific questions that weren't limited to Erica's time at work, he got answers that enabled him to act on her behalf.

2. **Focus on individual needs, goals, and struggles.** It's easy for leaders to track team or departmental results, but don't forget that individuals make up the whole. When your entire team performs at high levels, you may be tempted to spend less time with each person. Don't fall into this trap! Spend consistent time with individuals, regardless of team outcomes.

3. **Prioritize learning and professional development.** By definition, a mentor teaches, guides, and counsels. As a mentor, you provide opportunities for employees to progress in the organization and clarify what it takes to succeed in their professions and within the company.

HOW MENTORSHIP STRENGTHENS YOUR WORK CULTURE

Mentorship strengthens individuals, but it also multiplies organizational strength by developing future leaders. Teaching by example is good, but sometimes teaching by explanation is better. When you explain your decisions or debrief what happened in a meeting, you may be providing new insight to an employee who is considering a future in leadership. You can also let newer employees shadow more senior members of your team so they can see different interpersonal skills at play and clearly understand how to thrive within your company culture. Acquiring this type of knowledge early on builds confidence and sparks possibility. Employees begin to imagine an exciting future with your organization, because they've already started experiencing it.

Another way mentorship benefits work culture is by repurposing talent. Erica's husband, Matt, leads teams largely made up of millennials. In 2021, the Great Resignation affected his company, like many others, and turnover was higher than usual. Matt's leadership style incorporates coaching and mentorship. During a time when employees churned through jobs at alarming rates, Matt focused on building relationships with his team. He took the time to know them as professionals and learn about their personal lives. Matt invested time in each person to identify their skills and learn how to support them well. He fostered a strength-based culture so individuals, and his team, could thrive.

Matt's tactics were brilliantly innovative, if not a little surprising. If an employee's skills weren't a perfect fit for Matt's team, he didn't usher the person out the door. Instead, he transitioned them into a different department that needed their skills. This type of repurposing happened more than once, which lent stamina and stability to the overall company by reducing turnover and creating a living legacy of care and compassion. Matt's team remains one of the highest performing teams at the company today.[10] I believe one of the primary reasons for this success is Matt's ability to blend great mentoring with great leadership, a skill that has served employees and the company well.

MENTORING WOMEN YOU DON'T FORMALLY LEAD

When I was a corporate leader, I mentored women inside and outside the company. Significantly fewer women than men worked in our industry, and I felt compelled to offer women time, guidance, and advice. I wanted to be the mentor I never had.

In my situation, the chance to support women outside the company wasn't part of a formal program—it happened organically. As a board member of the Outdoor Industry Women's Coalition, I spoke about managing workplace change at a panel event. Afterward, a group of young women approached me. We had a brief conversation about change and then exchanged contact information. In the years that followed, we met and talked about their challenges, such as career advancement and conflict management. I found these interactions refreshing. In listening to them, giving them feedback, and encouraging them, I learned how to better serve my team. Helping these women grow professionally helped me develop as a leader.

Mentoring women who worked at other companies brought fewer

complications and distractions, not just for me, but for the mentees too. They felt comfortable because I was a detached outsider. Less investment was required of me because mentees would come and go as their problems came and went. We remained in contact after their issues resolved, but these relationships were different from those developed between me and the women on my team.

Women from inside the same company can also step into an informal mentoring role. Catherine shared with me how, early in her career, she benefited from a senior professional's informal mentorship. Marge and Catherine shared the same boss, who tasked Catherine with starting a new department. Marge intentionally poured time and guidance into Catherine, which was a huge confidence booster. When Catherine had to prepare the first business proposal she ever wrote, Marge gave her feedback and advice. Catherine recalls the impact this made on her as a young professional: it transformed her career. Marge's willingness to counsel her is another example of how mentoring can happen outside our own teams.

If you're wanting to mentor women who aren't your direct reports, here are seven tips to get you started:

1. Pray that God would guide you into mentorship opportunities.
2. Notice your sphere of influence. Look at your network, church, industry organization, friends, and community. Who might benefit from your guidance or support?
3. Be mindful, open, and obedient.
4. Start simple: Offer encouragement, invite someone to lunch, or just be willing to listen when someone has a problem.
5. Check in with someone you know is struggling professionally. Send a quick text or an email.

6. Be willing to share your own story. Being vulnerable about what you've overcome is often the most helpful wisdom you can offer.

7. Remember: Interactions may be long-term, seasonal, or even a single occurrence. God will use each one, no matter the duration.[11]

THREE CORE PRINCIPLES TO MENTOR WELL

Whether you're mentoring people inside or outside your team, here are three core principles to guide you:

Rely on the Holy Spirit for wisdom. Catherine talked to me about a time when she had to speak hard truth into someone's situation. At the end she said, "I'm off my soapbox now." The person responded, "You weren't on your soapbox. You were on your Spirit box!"[12] Regardless of how closely we work with someone, we can't know all the factors impacting them and the issue we're coaching them through. But the Holy Spirit knows. He grants us discernment so we know what to say, what questions to ask, and how best to help.

You can be genuine in your faith without being overwhelming. God is detailed, intentional, and specific. Following a routine script is performative and disingenuous. You don't need to pray with someone or quote the Bible during every interaction. As Catherine told me, "My faith is part of who I am. I don't need to challenge the other person's belief system or force mine."[13] We can authentically talk about God's involvement in our own experiences without making the other person feel uncomfortable.

Know what you're willing to offer. Mentees will approach you with a variety of needs. They may want to grasp how to live out their faith at work, or how to strengthen their leadership skills. A high-maintenance boss or coworker may be causing them stress, or they may want suggestions on how to balance life and work. Some mentees want to meet regularly, while others only want your involvement for the duration of their current challenge. Before agreeing to mentor someone, know the topics you're willing to tackle and how much time you're willing to invest.

SACRED WORK

Fifty men from the company of the prophets went and stood at a distance, facing the place where Elijah and Elisha had stopped at the Jordan. Elijah took his cloak, rolled it up and struck the water with it. The water divided to the right and to the left, and the two of them crossed over on dry ground. When they had crossed, Elijah said to Elisha, "Tell me, what can I do for you before I am taken from you?" "Let me inherit a double portion of your spirit," Elisha replied.

2 KINGS 2:7–9

I love that recycling faith and strength is an ancient biblical practice, and one of my favorite biblical examples of mentorship involves Elijah and Elisha. By the time God instructs Elijah to anoint Elisha as his successor, Elijah has gone before King Ahab multiple times, lives through a drought in isolation, miraculously provides for a widow woman in enemy territory, raises her son from the dead, and prays down God's fire to turn the people's hearts back to Him. Then he develops a terrible case of burnout and runs away, only to be comforted, revived, and encouraged by God (see 1 Kings 17–19).

Elijah carries forward all these experiences, these trials and triumphs of his faith, into his mentorship of Elisha. Scholars estimate that Elijah and his protégé spend about six years together before God mysteriously takes Elijah up to heaven in a whirlwind.[14] Afterward,

Elisha's work as a lone prophet closely resembles Elijah's, everything from the miracles he performs to the prophecies he makes and the confrontations he has with wicked men (see 2 Kings 2–13). Elijah's legacy—God's legacy—is only possible because he goes first and then pours into Elisha. In a similar way, God is always going first for us! We can grow strong and wise because He is strong and wise. He fills us with His Spirit so we can be like Him, and lead like Him.

As you experience leadership and faith challenges, count what God teaches you as legacy. He has gone before you and paved the way for you to walk in. Because the Holy Spirit lives within you, you are fully equipped to lead because you know who to follow. Go first, knowing He will recycle and repurpose what you learn in the lives and careers of your mentees.

Remember: God wastes nothing!

My prayer for you: Father, thank You for the leader reading these words. Thank You that she wants to give back. She isn't keeping the knowledge and experience You've given her for selfish gain; she wants to pass it on. Help her, Father, to know who and how You want her to mentor. Guide her timing and connect her to the person who needs her most. I pray that Your legacy of wisdom, strength, and comfort will flow through her and empower those she mentors.

Recommended Books for Women Leaders

The Confidence Cornerstone: A Woman's Guide to Fearless Leadership by Catherine Gates

God's Not Done with You: How to Advance Your Career and Live in Abundance by Mary E. Guirovich

Killing Comparison: Reject the Lie You Aren't Good Enough and Live Confident in Who God Made You to Be by Nona Jones

Real Women, Real Issues: Positive Collaborations for Business Success by Debra Gould, Nancy J. Lewis, Michelle Porchia, and Carole Copeland Thomas

sheWorks4Him: Embrace Your Calling as a Christian Woman at Work by Jim and Martha Brangenberg

Women & Work: Bearing God's Image and Joining in His Mission Through Our Work, a collective work edited by Courtney Moore

Work, Love, Pray: Practical Wisdom for Professional Christian Women and Those Who Want to Understand Them by Diane Paddison

Acknowledgments

Feeling incredibly grateful to—

My family:

George, whose big heart went all-in with me on this big book adventure. Thank you for supporting my dream, love.

My amazing daughter Larkin who wrote these words to me when I put away the business costume and picked up the pen: "Write away, right away, always."

Karen West, my tireless prayer warrior and encourager. We started out as twelve-year-olds singing on the school bus and forty-five years later, our hearts are still bound by the God who brought us together.

Jim and Kathy Brown, for seeing my little girl's heart and giving me a soft place to land when all the other doors closed.

Johnny and Sally Golding, whose trust in the Lord and unconditional love for me have had the greatest impact on my faith.

Donna, Ro, and Fran, my precious matriarchs whose fierce, tender hearts have restored my lost years. I could not feel more at home than I do with you.

A community of sage scribes:

The incredible, savvy team at Moody Publishers, with special gratitude to Trillia Newbell for being the first to believe in me and my book; Judy Dunagan for praying and guiding me through the process; and Pam Pugh whose artful editing and clever wit helped me bring the finish line into view.

Wendy Lawton, of Books & Such Literary Agency, for her wisdom and experience.

Lysa TerKeurst, for keeping her promise to God and founding Compel Training for fledgling writers.

Glynnis Whitwer, for coaching me through Compel's first-ever book proposal bootcamp.

Amy, Jessica, Leslie, and Rachel: We met during bootcamp and kept growing and going but best of all—together.

Jen Allee and Jessica Hanna, who asked all the right (hard) questions about my first draft and helped me find the perfect portions of clarity and pizzazz.

Those who walked, ran, and knelt beside me as this book came to be:

My mentors Betty Slade and Catherine Gates, for inspiring me in how you seek the Holy Spirit and then put feet to your faith.

All the men and women whose stories are woven around mine in this book and those who endorsed it. What a gift you gave me, and I am honored!

My beta reading team, who took hours out of their terribly busy lives to help forge this book into its best version. Special thanks to Mandy Johnson and the other writers: your insights kept me close to my readers when the writing process threatened to carry me away.

Michele Jan and Jen Chapman, who live leadership daily and still find time to read my words and cheer me on.

Nancy J. Lewis and the Tuesday night prayer warriors, whose faithful intercession sustained me.

My mustard-seed sisters: Becky, Cathy, Marianne, Pie, Stacie, and TJ. Spending time in God's Word with you as we share table fellowship is one of my greatest joys.

My team at Petzl:

Those were the best of times, and you were simply the best!

Notes

CHAPTER 1: RECOGNIZING AND OVERCOMING IMPOSTER SYNDROME

1. Nona Jones, *Killing Comparison: Reject the Lie You Aren't Good Enough and Live Confident in Who God Made You to Be* (Grand Rapids: Zondervan, 2022), 64.
2. "Imposter Syndrome," *Psychology Today*, https://www.psychologytoday.com/us/basics/imposter-syndrome.
3. Porter Braswell, "The Real Reason More Women and People of Color Suffer from Imposter Syndrome," *Fast Company*, March 21, 2023, https://www.fastcompany.com/90868279/imposter-syndrome-is-a-collective-burden-not-a-personal-problem.
4. Sheryl Nance-Nash, "Why Imposter Syndrome Hits Women of Colour Harder," BBC, July 27, 2020, https://www.bbc.com/worklife/article/20200724-why-imposter-syndrome-hits-women-and-women-of-colour-harder.
5. "2022 Women in the Workplace: Key Findings," Lean In, https://leanin.org/women-in-the-workplace#key-findings-2022.
6. Timothy Larsen, "Evangelicalism's Strong History of Women in Ministry," *Reformed Journal*, August 31, 2017, https://reformedjournal.com/evangelicalisms-strong-history-women-ministry/.
7. Staci Diffendaffer, *Unconditioned Love: Healing Hearts and Minds in a Time of Conflict and Division* (Winston-Salem: Southern Fried Karma LLC, 2021), 88.
8. Jones, 119.
9. Julie Tseng and Jordan Poppenk, "Brain Meta-state Transitions Demarcate Thoughts across Task Contexts Exposing the Mental Noise of Trait Neuroticism," *Nature Communications* 11, no. 3480 (July 13, 2020): 7, https://doi.org/10.1038/s41467-020-17255-9.

CHAPTER 2: MAKING DIFFICULT DECISIONS

1. John Cook, *The Book of Positive Quotations* (Minneapolis: Fairview Press, 1997), 310.
2. Darren A. Smith, "The One Leadership Quality That You Need: Decision-Making," *Forbes*, last modified December 9, 2021, https://www.forbes.com/sites/forbesbusinesscouncil/2021/12/09/the-one-leadership-quality-that-you-need-decision-making/?sh=1b3e48af3f59.
3. "Decision Making in the Age of Urgency," McKinsey & Company, last modified April 30, 2019, https://www.mckinsey.com/capabilities/people-and-organizational-performance/our-insights/decision-making-in-the-age-of-urgency.
4. Amy Lively, interview by author, December 9, 2022.
5. Therese Huston, "Are Women Better Decision Makers?" *The New York Times*, last modified October 17, 2014, https://www.nytimes.com/2014/10/19/opinion/sunday/are-women-better-decision-makers.html.
6. Huston, "Are Women Better Decision Makers?"
7. Mara Mather and Nichole R. Lighthall, "Risk and Reward are Processed Differently in Decisions Made Under Stress," *Current Directions in Psychological Science*, 21, no. 1 (January 21, 2012): 36–41, https://doi.org/10.1177/0963721411429452.
8. Christian Thöni and Stefan Volk, "Converging Evidence for Greater Male Variability in Time, Risk, and Social Preferences," *Proceedings of the National Academy of Sciences*, 118, no. 23 (June 4, 2021), https://doi.org/10.1073/pnas.2026112118.
9. Mather and Lighthall, 36–41.
10. Huston, "Are Women Better Decision Makers?"
11. Chris Bart and Gregory McQueen, "Why Women Make Better Directors," *International Journal of Business Governance and Ethics*, 8, no. 1 (March 21, 2013): 93–99, https://doi.org/10.1504/IJBGE.2013.052743.
12. Bart and McQueen, "Why Women Make Better Directors."
13. Ibid.
14. Cathy Benko and Bill Pelster, "How Women Decide," *Harvard Business Review*, last modified September 1, 2013, https://hbr.org/2013/09/how-women-decide.
15. Valerie van Mulukom, "Is It Rational to Trust Your Gut Feelings?," *Neuroscience News*, May 18, 2018, https://neurosciencenews.com/gut-feelings-9082.

16. Britannica, s.v. "Remez," *Encyclopedia Britannica*, https://www.britannica .com/topic/remez.
17. Ibid.
18. Ibid.

CHAPTER 3: MANAGING WORKPLACE CONFLICT

1. Philip Knight, quoted in Dan Spainhour, *Coach Yourself: A Motivational Guide for Coaches and Leaders* (Winston-Salem: Educational Coaching & Business Communications, 2007), 175.
2. Excerpt from author's personal journal, June 13, 2011.
3. Strong's H2534, *Blue Letter Bible*, https://www.blueletterbible.org/ lexicon/h2534/kjv/wlc/0-1/.
4. *Human Capital Report July 2008*, CPP Global, https://www.themyers briggs.com/-/media/f39a8b7fb4fe4daface552d9f485c825.ashx.
5. Catherine now serves as the vice president of business partnerships for the Polished Network.
6. Catherine Gates, interview by author, December 22, 2022.
7. Max Lucado, *When God Whispers Your Name* (Nashville: Thomas Nelson, 1999), 44.
8. The Holy Bible, New Century Version®. Copyright © 2005 by Thomas Nelson, Inc.
9. James Strong, *Strong's Exhaustive Concordance of the Bible* (Peabody, MA: Hendrickson Publishers, 1990), s.v. "rebuke."

CHAPTER 4: LEADING REMOTELY

1. Bryan Robinson, "Remote Work Is Here To Stay and Will Increase Into 2023, Experts Say," *Forbes*, last modified February 1, 2022, https://www .forbes.com/sites/bryanrobinson/2022/02/01/remote-work-is-here-to-stay-and-will-increase-into-2023-experts-say/?sh=318768d620a6.
2. "Remote Work Statistics [2022]: Facts, Trends, and Projections," Zippia, last modified April 5, 2022, https://www.zippia.com/advice/remote-work-statistics/.
3. Robinson, "Remote Work Is Here To Stay and Will Increase Into 2023, Experts Say."
4. "Culture: 4 Keys To Why It Matters," McKinsey & Company, accessed November 2, 2022, https://www.mckinsey.com/capabilities/people-and-organizational-performance/our-insights/the-organization-blog/culture-4-keys-to-why-it-matters.

5. The term *quiet quitting* became popular in 2022 and described employees who didn't formally quit their jobs but instead started doing only what was needed to get by. They mentally checked out or only performed the bare minimum.

6. Jeremy Bailenson, "Four Causes for 'Zoom Fatigue' and Their Solutions," *Stanford News*, last modified March 1, 2021, https://news .stanford.edu/2021/02/23/four-causes-zoom-fatigue-solutions/.

7. Bailenson, "Four Causes for 'Zoom Fatigue' and Their Solutions."

8. The term *The Great Resignation* describes what started in the spring of 2021 when droves of US workers began resigning from their jobs. During the pandemic, many people realized how unsatisfied they were with their jobs, so they quit in record numbers.

9. "SHRM Research Reveals Negative Perceptions of Remote Work," Society of Human Resource Management, last modified July 26, 2021, https:// www.shrm.org/about-shrm/press-room/press-releases/pages/-shrm-research-reveals-negative-perceptions-of-remote-work.aspx.

10. Society of Human Resource Management, "SHRM Research Reveals."

11. Strong's G2041, *Blue Letter Bible*, accessed February 8, 2023, https:// www.blueletterbible.org/lexicon/g2041/kjv/tr/0-1/.

12. Melissa Petruzzello, "St. Paul's Contributions to the New Testament," *Encyclopedia Britannica*, May 22, 2018, https://www.britannica.com/list/ st-pauls-contributions-to-the-new-testament.

13. "Common Forms of Transportation in the Ancient World," American Bible Society, https://bibleresources.americanbible.org/resource/ common-forms-of-transportation-in-the-ancient-world.

14. Valeriy A. Alikin, "Singing and Prayer in the Gathering of the Early Church," *The Earliest History of the Christian Gathering: Origin, Development and Content of the Christian Gathering in the First to Third Centuries* (Netherlands: Brill, 2010), 211–54, https://www.jstor.org/stable/ 10.1163/j.ctt1w76wv6.11.

CHAPTER 5: LEADING THROUGH CRISIS

1. Peter Seng, Introduction to *Synchronicity*, by Joseph Jaworski (Oakland, CA: Berrett-Koehler Publishers, 2011), 3.

2. "The Future of Work After COVID-19," McKinsey Global Institute, https://www.mckinsey.com/featured-insights/future-of-work/the-future-of-work-after-covid-19.

3. Aman Kidwai, "How Much Money Employers Can Save When They Switch to Remote or Hybrid Work," *Fortune*, August 15, 2022, https://fortune.com/2022/08/15/how-much-money-employers-save-switch-remote-hybrid-work/.

4. Jeanne Sahadi, "The Latest on Hybrid Work: Who Is WFH and Who Isn't," CNN, April 9, 2023, https://www.cnn.com/2023/04/09/success/hybrid-wfh-remote-work/index.html.

5. "2022 Women in the Workplace: Key Findings," Lean In, https://leanin.org/women-in-the-workplace#key-findings-2022.

6. Sara Jane Glynn, "Breadwinning Mothers Continue to Be the U.S. Norm," Center for American Progress, last modified May 10, 2019, https://www.americanprogress.org/issues/women/reports/2019/05/10/469739/breadwinning-mothers-continue-u-s-norm/.

CHAPTER 6: LEADING THROUGH CHANGE

1. John C. Maxwell (@officialjohnmaxwell), LinkedIn post, May 25, 2022, https://www.linkedin.com/posts/officialjohnmaxwell_any-time-there-is-change-there-is-opportunity-activity-6848209750509801472-7Ijp/?trk=public_profile_like_view.

2. Amy Lively, interview by author, December 9, 2022.

3. Ibid.

4. "How to Double the Odds That Your Change Program Will Succeed," McKinsey & Company, last modified August 29, 2019, https://www.mckinsey.com/capabilities/people-and-organizational-performance/our-insights/how-to-double-the-odds-that-your-change-program-will-succeed.

5. "Resistance to Change in Organizations Comes From These 5 Factors," Leadership IQ, last modified November 28, 2020, https://www.leadershipiq.com/blogs/leadershipiq/resistance-to-change-in-organizations-comes-from-these-5-factors-new-data.

6. Ibid.

7. Ibid.

8. "What Happened Between the Old and New Testaments?," Zondervan Academic, February 22, 2016, https://zondervanacademic.com/blog/what-happened-between-testaments.

9. Joanne Holstein, "Samaritan Woman at the Well," January 31, 2015, Guided Bible Studies for Hungry Christians, https://guidedbiblestudies.com/?p=2142.

10. Alyssa Roat, "The Samaritans: Hope from the History of a Hated People," Bible Study Tools, February 23, 2023, https://www.biblestudy tools.com/bible-study/topical-studies/the-samaritans-hope-from-the-history-of-a-hated-people.html.

CHAPTER 7: LEADING IN A MALE-DOMINATED INDUSTRY

1. Read about these women in Judges 4–5; the book of Esther; Acts 16:11–15, 40; Romans 16:1.
2. Catherine Gates, *The Confidence Cornerstone: A Women's Guide to Fearless Leadership* (Powell, OH: Author Academy Elite, 2020), 8.
3. "Women in Male-Dominated Industries and Occupations (Quick Take)," Catalyst, last modified January 21, 2022, https://www.catalyst.org/research/women-in-male-dominated-industries-and-occupations/.
4. Catalyst, "Women in Male-Dominated Industries."
5. Ibid.
6. "Occupations with the Smallest Share of Women Workers," U.S. Department of Labor, accessed November 19, 2022, https://www.dol.gov/agencies/wb/data/occupations/occupations-smallest-share-women-workers.
7. Mariela V. Campuzano, "Force and Inertia: A Systematic Review of Women Leadership in Male-Dominated Organizational Cultures in the United States," *Resource Development Review* 18, no. 4 (Dec. 2019): 437–69, https://doi.org/10.1177/1534484319861169.
8. Kim Parker, "Women in Majority-Male Workplaces Report Higher Rates of Gender Discrimination," Pew Research Center, last modified August 7, 2020, https://www.pewresearch.org/fact-tank/2018/03/07/women-in-majority-male-workplaces-report-higher-rates-of-gender-discrimination/.
9. Ibid.
10. Mikaela Kinder, "It's Time to Break the Cycle of Female Rivalry," *Harvard Business Review*, last modified April 14, 2020, https://hbr.org/2020/04/its-time-to-break-the-cycle-of-female-rivalry.
11. Campuzano, "Force and Inertia."
12. Diane Paddison, *Work, Love, Pray: Practical Wisdom for Professional Christian Women and Those Who Want to Understand Them* (Grand Rapids: Zondervan, 2011), 98.
13. "Judges: Importance and Role," Britannica, accessed December 10, 2022, https://www.britannica.com/topic/biblical-literature/Judges-importance-and-role.
14. Ibid.

CHAPTER 8: PROMOTING YOURSELF WITH CONFIDENCE

1. Mary E. Guirovich, interview by author, December 30, 2022.
2. Todd Wilson, "Mr. Milquetoast and Other Misconceptions About Humility," The Gospel Coalition, November 11, 2014, https://www.thegospelcoalition.org/article/mr-milquetoast-and-other-misconceptions-about-humility/.
3. Mary E. Guirovich, interview by the author, December 30, 2022.
4. Pamela Reynolds, "Women Don't Self-Promote, But Maybe They Should," Professional Development | Harvard DCE, last modified July 11, 2022, https://professional.dce.harvard.edu/blog/women-dont-self-promote-but-maybe-they-should/.
5. Christine Exley and Judd B. Kessler, "The Gender Gap in Self-Promotion," *National Bureau of Economic Research,* last modified May 2021, https://www.nber.org/papers/w26345.
6. Julio Mancuso, Ananta Neelim, and Joseph Vecci, "Gender Differences in Self-Promotion: Understanding the Female Modesty Constraint," *ResearchGate | Find and Share Research,* https://www.researchgate.net/publication/319944785_Self-Promotion_Social-Image_and_Gender_Inequality_Aiding_Women_Break_the_Shackles_of_Modesty.
7. Pamela Reynolds, "Women Don't Self-Promote." Also see Leihong Wang and Zhonggen Yu, "Gender-Moderated Effects of Academic Self-Concept on Achievement, Motivation, Performance, and Self-Efficacy," Frontiers in Psychology, 24, March 28, 2023: https://www.frontiersin.org/articles/10.3389/fpsyg.2023.1136141/full.
8. Mary E. Guirovich, *God's Not Done with You: How to Advance Your Career and Live in Abundance* (Austin, TX: Lioncrest Publishing, 2022), 217–25.
9. Mary E. Guirovich, interview by author, December 30, 2022.
10. Ibid.
11. The Common English Bible®, CEB® Copyright 2011 by Common English Bible.™

CHAPTER 9: NEGOTIATING TO WIN

1. Mary E. Guirovich, *God's Not Done with You: How to Advance Your Career and Live in Abundance* (Austin, TX: Lioncrest Publishing, 2022), 264.
2. Allison Doyle, "How Women Can Negotiate a Higher Salary and Close the Gender Gap," *The Balance,* last modified February 26, 2022, https://

www.thebalancemoney.com/strategies-for-women-to-negotiate-a-higher-salary-4067697.

3. Alexandra Mislin, "5 Tips for Women to Negotiate a Higher Salary," *Government Executive*, last modified March 14, 2023, https://www.govexec.com/workforce/2023/03/5-tips-women-negotiate-higher-salary/383948/.

4. Katie Shonk, "Women and Negotiation: Narrowing the Gender Gap in Negotiation," Program on Negotiation: Harvard Law School, April 6, 2023, https://www.pon.harvard.edu/daily/business-negotiations/women-and-negotiation-narrowing-the-gender-gap/.

5. Mara Olekalns, Ruchi Sinha, and Carol T. Kulik, Harvard Business Review, "3 of the Most Common Challenges Women Face in Negotiations," September 30, 2019, https://hbr.org/2019/09/3-of-the-most-common-challenges-women-face-in-negotiations.

6. Katie Shonk, "Women and Negotiation."

7. Erica Dvorak, interview by author, February 24, 2023.

8. Ibid.

9. Ibid.

10. "2023 Gender Pay Gap Report," Payscale, accessed May 23, 2023, https://www.payscale.com/research-and-insights/gender-pay-gap/#module-2.

11. Stephen Miller, "Gender Pay Gap Improvement Slowed During the Pandemic," Society of Human Resource Management, last modified March 15, 2022, https://www.shrm.org/resourcesandtools/hr-topics/compensation/pages/gender-pay-gap-improvement-slowed-during-the-pandemic.aspx.

CHAPTER 10: WHEN YOU FAIL

1. John Cook, *The Book of Positive Quotations* (Minneapolis: Fairview Press, 1997), 516.

2. Leslie McCleod, e-mail message to author, December 19, 2022.

3. Donald R. Keough, *The Ten Commandments for Business Failure* (New York: Penguin Group, 2011), 94.

4. Tom Peters, *The Pursuit of Wow! Every Person's Guide to Topsy-Turvy Times* (New York: Vintage Books, 1994), 4.

5. Author's personal journal, February 7, 2014.

CHAPTER 11: WHEN YOU AND YOUR BOSS DISAGREE

1. Catherine Gates, interview by author, December 22, 2022.
2. Ibid.
3. Staci Diffendaffer, e-mail message to author, November 10, 2022.
4. Ibid.
5. Strong's H1847, *Blue Letter Bible*, accessed May 28, 2023, https://www
.blueletterbible.org/lexicon/h1847/nasb20/wlc/0-1/.
6. Ibid.

CHAPTER 12: WHEN YOU'RE BETRAYED AT WORK

1. "Betrayed in the Workplace? 7 Steps for Healing," Center for Creative
Leadership, last modified March 18, 2021, https://www.ccl.org/articles/
leading-effectively-articles/betrayed-workplace-7-steps-healing/.
2. Interview with C-suite employee, November 11, 2022.
3. Ibid.
4. Erica Dvorak, interview by the author, March 2, 2023.

CHAPTER 13: WHEN YOU'RE PASSED OVER FOR A PROMOTION

1. Dietrich Bonhoeffer, *Letters and Papers from Prison* (Minneapolis: Fortress Press, 2015), 367–68.
2. Anonymous interview by author, February 27, 2023.
3. Ibid.
4. Kayla White, "The Legal Status of Barren Wives in the Ancient Near East,"
Priscilla Papers 28, no. 4 (Autumn 2014), https://www.cbeinternational
.org/resource/legal-status-barren-wives-ancient-near-east/.

CHAPTER 14: WHEN YOU NEED TO ADDRESS PERFORMANCE

1. John Cook, *The Book of Positive Quotations* (Minneapolis: Fairview
Press, 1997), 431.
2. Meredith Wholley, "17 Mind-Blowing Employee Engagement, Performance Review, and Performance Management Statistics," ClearCompany,
last modified July 14, 2022, https://blog.clearcompany.com/mind-
blowing-statistics-performance-reviews-employee-engagement.

CHAPTER 15: HOW TO BUILD A CULTURE
THAT ATTRACTS AND RETAINS TALENT

1. Nancy J. Lewis, interview by author, March 21, 2023.
2. Pragya Agarwal, "How to Create a Positive Workplace Culture," *Forbes*, accessed March 1, 2023, https://www.forbes.com/sites/pragyaagarwal europe/2018/08/29/how-to-create-a-positive-work-place-culture/?sh= 5d988c4d4272.
3. "Global Culture Survey 2021," PricewaterhouseCoopers, accessed March 1, 2023, https://www.pwc.com/gx/en/issues/upskilling/global-culture-survey-2021.html.
4. PricewaterhouseCoopers, "Global Culture Survey 2021."
5. LinkedIn poll with industry leaders (anonymous), February 9, 2022.
6. Evan Tarver, "Corporate Culture Definition: Characteristics and Importance Explained," *Investopedia*, last modified December 22, 2022, https://www.investopedia.com/terms/c/corporate-culture.asp.
7. "5 Culture Trends for 2023," O.C. Tanner—Appreciate Great Work, https://www.octanner.com/insights/white-papers/5-culture-trends-for-2023.html.
8. Anonymous interviews with human resource professionals by author, March 6–10, 2023.
9. Sara Korolevich, "Horrible Bosses: A Survey of the American Workforce," GoodHire, last modified January 11, 2022, https://www.goodhire.com/resources/articles/horrible-bosses-survey/.
10. Arthur Satterwhite, "Christians Should Lead the Way in Diversity and Equity," *Christianity Today*, May 11, 2022, https://www.christianitytoday.com/ct/2022/may-web-only/diversity-equity-evangelical-christian-youth-ministry.html.
11. Nancy J. Lewis, interview by author, March 21, 2023.
12. Ibid.
13. Labor Force Statistics from the Current Population Survey 2022, accessed May 6, 2023, https://www.bls.gov/cps/cpsaat03.htm.
14. Nancy J. Lewis, interview by author, March 21, 2023.
15. Kristi McLelland, "The Gospel on the Ground," filmed 2022, Session 1, Lifeway Press, video, 32:24.
16. Ray Vander Laan, "Rabbi and Talmidim," That the World May Know, https://www.thattheworldmayknow.com/rabbi-and-talmidim.

CHAPTER 16: THE POWER OF MENTORSHIP

1. Quotes of J Loren Norris published by others, accessed August 10, 2023, https://www.jlorennorris.com/media.html.
2. Catherine now serves as the vice president of business partnerships for the Polished Network.
3. Merriam-Webster.com Dictionary, s.v. "mentor," accessed March 15, 2023, https://www.merriam-webster.com/dictionary/mentor.
4. Collins English Dictionary, s.v. "mentor," accessed March 15, 2023, https://www.collinsdictionary.com/us/dictionary/english/mentor.
5. Catherine Gates, interview by author, December 22, 2022.
6. "Leaders vs. Mentors: Traits and Differences," indeed, last modified June 24, 2022, https://www.indeed.com/career-advice/career-development/leader-vs-mentor.
7. Indeed, "Leaders vs. Mentors: Traits and Differences."
8. Ibid.
9. Marianna Tu and Michael Li, "What Great Mentorship Looks Like in a Hybrid Workplace," *Harvard Business Review*, last modified May 12, 2021, https://hbr.org/2021/05/what-great-mentorship-looks-like-in-a-hybrid-workplace.
10. Erica Dvorak, interview by author, March 2, 2023.
11. Gates, 2022 and Dvorak, 2023.
12. Gates, 2022.
13. Ibid.
14. Clarence L. Haynes Jr., "Who Are Elijah and Elisha in the Bible?" Biblestudytools.com, last modified February 18, 2022, https://www.biblestudytools.com/bible-study/topical-studies/who-are-elijah-and-elisha-in-the-bible.html.

sacred work.

Providing free mentorship and resources for Christian women who work and lead in the marketplace.

Join the Sacred Work email community, where we'll explore the intersection between faith and work while equipping you to show up boldly in both spaces. Bimonthly editions include:

- Relevant topics that impact professional Christian women
- Scripture-based guidance around these topics
- Book recommendations and giveaways
- Opportunities for collaboration, connection, and mentorship
- Free print and video resources to support you in the marketplace

www.peggybodde.com